TOO BIG TO THINK

TOO BIG TO THINK

AN ENGLISHMAN, A SMALL
NORWEGIAN TOWN, AND
THEIR WAR AGAINST THE
GERMAN AUTO GIANTS

ROGER COCKROFT

MANUSCRIPTS
PRESS

TOO BIG TO THINK

An Englishman, a Small Norwegian Town, and Their War against the German Auto Giants

ISBN   979-8-88926-853-6 *Paperback*
        979-8-88926-854-3 *eBook*
        979-8-88926-855-0 *Hardcover*

To my children Victoria, Benjamin, and Hugo,

for forgiving my five-year absence from your childhood.

To Charlotte Cockroft, for letting friendship overcome tragedy.

To Hilde Rullestad, for saving my life in so many different ways.

To the community of Farsund for adopting me.

But most of all to Martin Roth, for being a predictable arsehole.

Contents

"If the enemy is within range, so are you."

"To know your enemy, you must become your enemy."

Main Characters

FARSUND

Henrique Adao: director of new projects for the factory

Rune Almas: operations director for the factory

Dr. Reza Babaei: head of casting simulation

Richard Buch: mayor of Farsund after Stein Ytterdahl

Per Erik: senior process engineer and Kristen Ommundsen's boss

Frank Edvinsen: production supervisor for the factory

Helge Fait: HR director for the factory

Almar Friestad: industry liaison officer for Farsund Kommune

Grethe Hindersland: original plant manager under Alcoa

Tim Lima: finance guy hired by Congaree Capital

Dr. Jan Ove Loland: head of research and development

Karsten Mohr: sales director for the factory

Gordon Moskaland: purchasing manager for the factory

Knut Nesvold: finance guy who replaces Tim Lima

Kristen Ommundsen: process engineer for the factory

Knut Pettersen: head of quality department

Hilde Rullestad: logistics manager for the factory

Stein Ytterdahl: mayor of Farsund

CONGAREE CAPITAL PARTNERS/"MONEY MEN"
Kentucky Kyle/Kyle Crammer: operations partner

Bob Baker: managing partner

Stanley Cuttle: operations associate

THE GOVERNMENT ADMINISTRATION TEAM
Håvard Wiker: partner and administrator of the Bankruptcy Estate

Erik Sandtrø: junior partner and assistant to Håvard Wiker

PORSCHE/VOLKSWAGEN

Karin Degler: director of risk management and Martin Roth's understudy

Holger Härter: CFO of Porsche and Wendelin Wiedeking's sidekick

Michael Macht: interim CEO after Wendelin Wiedeking

Matthias Muller: replacement CEO after Michael Macht

Martin Roth: head of risk management

Francisco Javier García Sanz: head of the supply chain for VW group

Stephen Spreiter: head of purchasing

Wendelin Wiedeking: CEO of Porsche AG

BMW

Dr. Herbert Diess: member of board of management, head of supply chain, and later CEO of VW group

Philip-Christian Eller: member of board of management and head of purchasing

Peter Gaehrken: senior buyer for purchasing

Joachim Goldbach: vice president of purchasing

Reinhold Hierl: manager reporting to Frank Solbach

Harald Hoschek: manager who replaces Reinhold Hierl and later Frank Solbach

Alois Rankl: head of quality for BMW Dingolfing, one of BMW's largest production facilities

Hans Saller: buyer for BMW

Jurgen Schleinitz: senior legal counsel

Frank Solbach: senior purchasing manager

Prologue

———

MAY 25, 2009
MUNICH, GERMANY
The phone went dead. The pirate had hung up.

A cocktail of emotions swirled around the room: anxiety, shock, humiliation. Most of all, though, anger coursed through the veins of the Germans. They were the giants of the automotive world, the most powerful men in a cutthroat industry. Yet a thousand miles away, in a small Norwegian town called Farsund, that petulant pirate had just threatened to starve them of their unique supply of parts if they didn't do exactly as he said. One man would stop all of them from making cars.

This meeting room in Munich represented the center of BMW's powerhouse—the FIZ. It matched the genre of the hosts, perfectly functional and clinically clean but lacking any style. Two Germans and one Italian were the main characters who huddled around an oversized meeting table. Its light brown, grained wood finish had been worn down over the years, but it was the best BMW could offer. Besides, the table complemented the maroon fabric chairs. All offered a bland taste of the late '80s.

Nothing in the room matched the image of the Italian guest, Luca Vezzani. His thick, black hair was stylishly cut and swept back. It gave him a vibrant yet sophisticated look matching his handsome face and sultry eyes. He was well-dressed too. A dark Italian tailored suit and crisp white shirt staged his deep red silk tie. He embodied Ferrari in every sense.

Until this point, he had worked closely with his counterparts from BMW and Porsche. But now things had changed. They all wanted the Norwegian factory to supply parts, but their objectives diverged. BMW needed it alive just long enough to supply the few remaining parts required to finish a model year build of one of the most prestigious cars in their fleet. Porsche had a different problem. The factory had to make their parts for a much longer time, so they wanted it taken by a new owner, someone they trusted who would willingly comply with Porsche's rules. Neither had expected such pushback from an outsider. It had caught them off guard and exposed them to the real threat of losing billions of dollars—not a message any of them wanted to convey to their respective CEOs.

Vezzani took a deep breath and pushed away from the table. His accent was strong, but his English was clear and precise. "Gentlemen, Ferrari is out. This is just too expensive."

As he uttered those decisive words, Vezzani gazed directly across the table at Frank Solbach of BMW. Solbach had survived the majority of his career in the company, but the toll it took showed. Dodging political bullets had thinned and *grayed his hair, which he plastered down to cover his bony skull. Yet this felt like a small price to pay for his current position: master manipulator within the BMW machine. Frank Solbach wielded real power, though not the loud and aggressive kind. Stealth was his weapon of choice. He could fit into any meeting, adapt to any setting, and make himself invisible. Like a hawk, he would observe silently before swooping in at just the right moment.*

But today was different. His authority had, for once, been undermined—first by that upstart pleb in Norway, and now by this flashy Italian. The latter had taken his cue from the former. Both had disobeyed the pecking order, blatantly ignoring the fact BMW was the biggest force in the room. Solbach had offered the Italian a place in his solution. He had been kind; benevolent, even. He had promised to protect Ferrari and ensure their precious supply of parts would be maintained, but only under the might BMW represented. So Vezzani's decision to walk away came as an embarrassing insult. This would have to be reported to the uppermost BMW executives, raising questions about BMW's authority and Solbach's ability to deal with risks.

Solbach cast a piercing glare through his gold-rimmed glasses and then spat out his final words: "Are you sure, Mr. Vezzani? Are you sure you want to jeopardize the future of Ferrari?" His shrill tone carried the depth of his disgust.

Now it was Martin Roth's turn to step in, representing Porsche. He was dressed in the finest German executive wardrobe, black suit and thin black tie against a plain white shirt. But he didn't fit the Porsche style. He looked like an angry hog stuffed into that suit. His jowls puffed out, and his eyes were red, accentuating his anger. His curly brown hair looked messy, more in line with his swine-like appearance than the image of crisp German efficiency. He didn't care. Protecting Porsche was his number-one priority, especially now when his CEO was on the verge of a miracle power play.

Porsche had long been an underdog in the car-making world, not even the biggest in their hometown of Stuttgart, Germany. Plans had been afoot, though. If Roth's bosses pulled off their devious stunt to buy Volkswagen, Porsche would become the biggest car maker in the world. The deal would put them—not BMW—at the head of every table. In order for this plot to succeed, Roth needed to make sure nothing went wrong, which meant everyone in the room had to combine forces against their Norwegian enemy.

With his thick German accent, Roth slowly repeated Solbach's warning, "This will not be a cheap option for you, Mr. Vezzani. You will end up paying much more if you choose to leave us now. You can't have thought this through." Roth made clear his intent to punish Vezzani and Ferrari if they fell for the pirate's ploy and broke their automotive solidarity.

Yet Vezzani intended exactly that. He knew the threat to Ferrari was enormous, whichever route he took. BMW and Porsche would wreak revenge if he left them, but the threat from Norway was even greater. If the Norwegian factory cut them off from these precious parts, they would have to completely stop production. They would lose about $1.6 billion in revenue until they found another parts supplier. This would surely bankrupt the company, especially then, in the aftermath *of the global financial crisis when money was tight. But Vezzani knew Ferrari had inventory stored away. They had enough parts to survive for three months—more time than Porsche or BMW had.*

They would have to solve this problem on their own. If they didn't, if the Norwegian factory closed its doors for good, Porsche wouldn't be able to launch their new model Panamera for three years, and BMW wouldn't be able to finish the build of their current 5 series model. That meant each of them faced losses of over $3 billion. It was definitely not Ferrari's problem—yet.

This fiasco stemmed from the Germans' own arrogance, a misguided belief corporations like theirs were immune from consequences; that they were far too established, far too important, and far "too big to fail." In reality, they were far too big to think. Now a pirate held them hostage. Either they pay him millions and millions of dollars, or he would make them lose billions.

Vezzani saw this challenger wasn't trying to swindle them. Solbach had forced the pirate into a desperate position, so his only intent was to save a factory and the people who depended on it. Vezzani knew those types of challengers fought hard with an unflagging resolve that matched the Ferrari spirit.

The phone call galvanized his decision. He had no interest in involving the great name of Ferrari in that mess. He couldn't help his curiosity, though. Who was this mysterious little pirate? It was obvious what he was trying to achieve, but how would he do it? And why did he care?

Vezzani turned as he exited the meeting room. "Gentleman, I'm excited to see how you both resolve this." Then he made a slight bow and politely uttered, "Scemi (Idiots)," as if it were a kind farewell.

CHAPTER 1

The Little Pirate

1974–2003
UK TO US
Summer 1974
Cam, Gloucestershire, UK

The latch on the dining room window was loose, just enough. Maureen jiggled the window and convinced it to slide open, but only a few inches before it jarred against the frame. Stubborn, it would budge no more. The gap was too small for my older brother Dave and barely big enough for my six-year-old body to squeeze through. Yet I somehow managed to pull myself past the frame as the other two pushed me from the outside. I tumbled onto a heap of dirty laundry, one of many abandoned piles festering in the dining room. I was in.

Mum had forgotten we'd gone for a walk and had accidentally locked the back door. She must have taken a mid-morning nap, which she did often. Peering past the open dining room door, I could see straight into the hallway. And there was Mum, lying on the tiled floor, completely asleep.

"Mummy's gone to sleep on the floor!" I shouted.

Maureen, a daughter from Mum's first marriage, had been looking after us. I knew little about Maureen. She was much older than me and Dave, and it didn't feel like she was related to us. Mum's other lives were a mystery to my brother and me.

"Yuck! Mummy's been sick all over the floor. I think she had porridge with a lot of honey. It smells sticky."

"Can you open the back door?" Maureen asked. I sidestepped Mum and her pool of vomit as I went to the back door, but I couldn't open it. The key had been removed from the lock. She hadn't wanted us to get in. I could open the front door though. It had a latch, and I knew how to use it.

Once opened, Maureen rushed in and instructed, "Go and play with your brother. Outside." I didn't go outside, though. I just watched as Maureen checked Mum and then made a phone call.

The ambulance arrived ten minutes later with sirens blaring and lights flashing bright blue. It was normally quiet in the Cotswold countryside, but the emergency crew knew Mum already. They'd been there before. It wouldn't be the last time either. Depression mixed with rum and opioids will do that to you.

Soon enough, I witnessed how quickly those substances not only destroy the addict but also burn through money. Mum ran up debts, which dwarfed what Dad could earn. He had to find a better-paying job and live away from home during the week. Maureen eventually left, so the only quasi-normal time was when Dad returned.

When he wasn't there, we had no structure and no boundaries. For years we didn't go to school. Then on Friday nights, Dad would show up with a comforting meal of fish and chips. On Saturday mornings, Dave and I would work with him to tidy up the filthy pit of our home. A week's worth of dirty dishes overflowed in the kitchen sink. No clothes had been washed. We didn't have any food either.

I loved teaming up with Dad to make things right, even if just for the weekend. I loved helping clean the house. I loved going shopping with him. I loved fixing problems. He never gave in. He gave me hope that "better" existed.

By the time I turned seven, Dad brought his elderly aunty to live with us. Mum was no good, and Aunty needed to be cared for. So I learned to cook. I also learned to stitch on buttons, mow the lawn, clean the house, and wash clothes. Looking after Aunty felt rewarding—to care for someone the way I wished Mum would have cared for us.

I started to grasp something: I couldn't be a spectator of bad. I couldn't be like Mum. I had to be rock solid and dependable, totally trustworthy for those who needed me. And I could not rest until I had proven I was good enough; until I had cleaned up the mess.

In 1978 my brother became a teenager. Dad was focused on rescuing our childhood. He moved the family to the

Midlands and sent us to a boarding school in Stourbridge. It got us away from Mum, and I loved it. Everyone appeared equal. We all wore the same uniform. Meals were provided regularly. Clothes were laundered. Sheets were clean. I thrived and grew. Suddenly I was a six-foot-three twelve-year-old. I constantly played rugby. I was big, tough, and invincible, or so I believed.

One day as I ascended the main staircase leading to the dormitories, I bumped into a man wearing a tweed suit and tie. He stood in my way, so I shifted over on the big staircase. But he blocked me again. He was short and slight, with round, silver-rimmed glasses. I looked down at him even though he stood a step above me. He had no intention of letting me pass.

In a firm tone, he said, "I'm here to talk to you, Mr. Cockroft." He didn't shout, but it was clear he was angry. "I am Mr. Boyce and you…" He poked me in the chest. "Are a bully."

He kept on stabbing my chest with his finger to emphasize his words. I towered so far above him he had to reach up to poke me. "I will fight you myself if you even touch my son again."

He stated this with such conviction, such courage, I could find no words to respond. As he brushed past me, I just stood there trying to digest what had happened. I was astounded. I wasn't a bully. His son, Ian, had a bed in my dormitory. Sure, we messed around, but I didn't hurt him. We had a game called Pull-a-Boyce. We'd grab his hair and run him down the dorm. Right at the end we'd slam him into the door. But it was only a joke. We'd occasionally put another padlock on his wardrobe so he couldn't open it. But that, too, was just a joke. One time I watched a kid punch Ian until he cried. I didn't do anything. It wasn't my issue. It was all in good fun.

Denial doesn't like to be interrupted. Mr. Boyce made sure it was. *Oh my god, who am I? What am I doing? What would it be like if I were to live in Ian's shoes?* The first to wake up every day, terrified of being beaten, not able to trust anyone, never letting my guard down. Then, the last to fall asleep at the end of the day, lying in bed, surrounded by thugs who might throw a late-night attack at any time.

I was inflicting torture on someone smaller than me simply for my own amusement. Ian's dad was right: I was nothing more than a big, horrible bully. The entire time, I had convinced myself I was a good guy. I had become complacent, not realizing how easy it was to commit and perpetuate wrongdoing. Dad would be ashamed of me. I had to stop who I'd become.

My encounter with that man marked the first time I truly questioned my sense of self. The second happened during the summer of 1986 when it came time to see if I'd graduated high school. Back then in the UK, graduation rested entirely on three or four final exams—"A" levels—which would test everything you'd been taught in the previous years. If you didn't pass those exams, you had two choices: spend another year to retake the exams or flunk out—a high school drop-out.

I'd already failed the first time. This was my second attempt. It was time to see if I'd passed—my last chance. I reasoned to myself that I would get through these exams and move to university, but who was I kidding? I hadn't spent any time studying. I partied too hard. Dad had even given me a sports car. I belonged to the "it crowd." There really wasn't time to study. Studying simply got in the way.

July rolled around, and the results were in. I headed into the college, where I picked up a plain, brown envelope with my name written starkly on the front. I walked to the edge of the parking lot, made sure I was alone, and opened it. The results were dreadful.

In front of me, the ground fell away steeply for about a hundred feet, and the Dudley Bowl stretched out for miles. This had been the home of the Industrial Revolution during the eighteenth century. Back then, thousands of factories had swallowed up thousands of boys every year and, if those boys were lucky, spat them back out at the end of each day. They labored under merciless conditions until finally, as old broken men, they retired to live among the smoke and machines that had become their community. These brave foot soldiers were the heroes of the revolution, bearers of progress. But at what price? Was I also going to join this struggle, oiling the wheels of the industrial machine?

I went home and talked to Dad. He was a nuclear physicist from Cambridge University, the sort of man who could answer any question you had straight off the bat without a moment of doubt. If Dad said something, you just knew it was true. Yet he was also a kind and gentle giant, with a hulking six-foot-five-inch frame, over three hundred pounds, silver hair, and piercing blue eyes. My dream had always been to make him proud; to find a way to study at Cambridge like him. I loved my dream, but I had never put in the effort. Now I faced disaster. We spent that evening trying to piece together a credible plan for my future.

Night fell. I couldn't sleep as I chewed through what I faced. The following day, around noon, Dad called from his office to tell me he could get me into a foundation apprentice course in Dudley College. If I was lucky and passed the apprenticeship, I'd have a job operating a lathe, cutting metal for the rest of my life. I was going to become part of the industrial machine through complacency, exactly as I'd feared.

My hope of being a high flier was all but over. In despair, I picked up the local paper and saw an advertisement offering people a second chance at education. The ad stated if your grades had let you down, then Birmingham Polytechnic—a second-tier version of a university—would help build you back up. My grades weren't just weak. They were catastrophic. But I figured I had nothing to lose, so I dialed the hotline number.

Peter Church answered. This was the man who might just hold the keys to my future. He was extremely polite but pointed out the obvious: I was a screwup with no track record of academic achievement. Somehow, though, I persuaded him to give me a chance. He invited me in for a meeting the next morning.

Peter was tall and thin, with an instantly likable face and a manner to match. As we sat in his office, he listened patiently as I tried to explain why I'd messed up before and why this time would be different. Reluctantly he offered me one last chance. I had to take an entrance exam for a diploma course in engineering. He'd let me in if I could pass an exam—much harder than the ones I'd repeatedly failed. I had only two weeks to prepare.

I'd heard the expression about taking a shot from the last chance saloon—and here I was, ordering doubles. I shut myself away and studied day and night. Occasionally I'd look out the window at one of the most beautiful summers the UK had seen for many years. The wind would catch the leaves of the trees, rustling them and beckoning me to join. I'd think about all the fun I was missing. Then the harsh reality of my situation hit me again. This was my final chance to get things right. Every minute counted.

At last the day arrived. After being shown into the exam room, I sat down at an old-school desk that had been used for many years. Countless scribbles adorned its surface. Peter wished me luck and handed me the exam paper. I had three hours.

The clock ticked methodically, and time shot past with question after question, all math, and all complex problems. Those three hours felt like mere seconds. The examiner told me to put my pen down. *Oh god, did I do enough?*

Peter called me the next day.

"I don't know how you did it, Mr. Cockroft, but you scored ninety-eight percent. Congratulations."

I was admitted, but on a ten-week probation. If I flunked anything within that period, I'd get kicked out. It didn't matter. The whole experience had taught me one of the most fundamental lessons in my life. Know what failure is. Know what it tastes like, what it feels like, and what it smells like. But remember, you only fail if you stop trying. If you don't try with 100 percent of your effort, you will never be 100 percent of who you could be. You can only take out what you put in. That's the thing about life: You learn the lesson only after the experience.

Like my father, I met my true love, Charlotte, in school. In those days, the engineering world was almost an exclusively male society, and we rarely interacted with females. But one December afternoon, I decided I wanted to get out of the boring engineering department and find another canteen across campus for lunch. I went exploring, just to be somewhere else.

I walked across the school quadrangle and saw two girls dressed up in sexy Santa outfits: high heels, short skirts, stockings and all. I swallowed, trying to maintain my composure as I saw them approaching me.

"We're holding our Christmas party this Thursday." Charlotte delved into her Christmas sack and pulled out a ticket. "Do you want to buy a ticket?" Our eyes met. We just stared at each other. She was mesmerizing, with deep engaging eyes, a creamy complexion, bright red lips, and an unmistakable elegance.

"Charlotte, are you going to do this all day? Or are you going to sell him some tickets?" her friend chimed in, breaking our gaze.

"Umm, sure. I'll buy four." I figured I could bring my friends for moral support.

We dated at first, just friends. She told me she never wanted to love anyone. She had enough love in her life already. Yet I could see the sadness in her eyes. She'd lost too many in her family.

A year later, we were sitting at a bar celebrating my twenty-first birthday. We were spitting peanuts at each other but barely managing through our laughter. Then she leaned into me. I could hardly hear her over the music.

"I love you."

I didn't know what to say. I think I loved her from the moment I met her, or pretty shortly after. But I never told her. Could I tell her now? Or would it scare her off?

"Well, that must be nice for you." Shock, followed by giggles of laughter.

We got married a week after I graduated.

Newly wed and fresh out of school, I landed my first job at Land Rover outside Birmingham. I was obsessed with cars, so working in the industry felt like a dream. Soon enough, I devised a plan to schedule all the deliveries from suppliers to the factory. I made our trucks pick up from different suppliers so they got really full too. We needed fewer trucks, and they waited less time to get unloaded. It made them more efficient and saved Land Rover about $60 million each year. My improvements then got the attention of Toyota in Derbyshire. They grabbed me to help build their European operations. There, we set a record for the fastest launch of a new vehicle in the whole global Toyota organization. I was steadily gaining a deeper understanding of exactly how car companies worked.

By the end of 1994 my career seemed to be thriving. But at this time Dad got very ill, the victim of a simultaneous stroke and heart attack. On April 9, 1995, I sat with him as he rested in bed. We'd been talking all afternoon. I was offered two new jobs and wasn't sure which one to take. Both were well-paid, and both would lead to exciting opportunities.

We'd gone over all the details, discussed the ins and outs of my options. But like he always did, Dad made sure to return to the bigger picture to regain perspective. "I'm so proud of both you and your brother. I talk to my colleagues about our children. They always say one of their children is doing really well. The other is artistic or special. What they really mean is they've got a problem child. Failure to launch is a real risk for them. But when I talk about you and Dave, I always say one son is doing really well and the other son is doing really well too."

Then he looked at me, pride in his eyes, and said something I'll never forget. "You're going to go all the way, aren't you?"

"I'm going to try, Dad. I don't know where I'll get to, but I promise it will be as far as I can."

He had a smile on his face. "I'll always be watching you."

He died that night at the age of fifty-one.

The following morning, my brother and I went to the solicitor's office to sort out Dad's affairs. Dad had died with little preparation, so Dave and I had to protect Mum from day one. We just didn't know what Dad had, and we were about to find out. As I stared out the office window, I thought I saw him walking in the street below, looking up at me.

Our first problem became abundantly clear. We couldn't trust those Dad had fought for. He'd built his own business focused on highly complex problem-solving machines testing everything: the recoil from a helicopter gun ship; the inside of nuclear reactors; the strength a pill needed to survive its life in a bottle. If you wanted to test something, Dad was your man. The company was his pride and joy. So when it fell into financial difficulty, he borrowed money against our home to secure the business and made sure people still got paid.

But as soon as Dad got ill, his once-loyal management began plotting against him. The second he died, they swung their plan into action: spend all the factory's money and stop collecting payments from customers. In other words, let it go bankrupt. Meanwhile, they had already struck a deal with a competitor. After crashing the company, they'd steal the customers and the order book. Then they'd jump ship to their new company and watch Dad's memory sink behind them. They figured all their suppliers would get paid and be happy to support them. The debt would go away too. The bank would get Dad's home, which they knew he had bet on for his business. They had no qualms about leaving Mum penniless.

They knew everything Dad had was tied up. He died intestate, which meant everything was frozen—all his money, assets, and most importantly, all his shares in the company… or, so they thought.

One small hole was in their otherwise airtight plan, one thing they didn't figure on: the Cockroft fighting spirit. After doing some research I discovered Dad had given Mum a single share, a pure token gesture. But it was registered, genuine, and the only share that could be used.

I found a lawyer. We worked on documents, which gave me the right to that one share. Mum conceded.

Next I called in Dad's three-person management team—Jill, James, and Jack—for an emergency general meeting. They had no idea what was coming. Dave and I sat in the meeting room, which resembled a greenhouse with windows looking out over the factory floor where all the machines now sat idle.

Once we all were assembled, I launched my attack. We talked about the dreadful state of the business and the financial situation. We talked about the commitments my father still had. We talked about the need to devise a productive way forward. They delivered their opening salvo: They had a buyer interested in the business. They didn't realize I already knew about their devious plot.

"Can you tell me who the buyer is, please? I'd like to meet them." I was polite and professional in my manner.

Jill, Dad's office manager and someone he once considered part of his family, spoke first, with an air of uncertainty in her voice. "Well, this is a business matter, and with all due respect, you're not part of the business. Look here." She pointed to the share certificate ledger she'd brought to the meeting. "I'm the company secretary, and I don't see your name in this register." Her voice steadied with her statement, the ledger seeming to firm up her resolve.

James, Dad's technical understudy, piped in. "You see, Roger, all your dad's shares in the company are tied up in his trust. You have no control in this business. Why don't you just leave this to us?" He had a smug expression. His eyes gleamed, and his cheeks flushed as though he was full of the anticipation of a victory.

I paused and then reached for my briefcase. I pulled out the letter I had Mum sign before the meeting. "Let me read this letter to you, if I may."

All three of them nodded. My heart was racing, but I couldn't show any fear or doubt.

"To whom it may concern, I am the owner of a single share in my late husband's company. I have gifted the share and all the rights to my son, Roger Cockroft."

The look of shock hadn't arrived yet. They were still confused about what this meant.

Without changing my tone, I resumed, "Now, I do know this meeting includes all those needed for a shareholder to call an emergency general meeting. That's what I am now doing, as the sole shareholder in the room." Bewilderment continued.

"First item on the agenda: I would like to propose Roger Cockroft is allowed to buy five shares in the company for the princely sum of five pounds. All those in favor?" I put my hand up. "All those against? Wait, I'm the only shareholder, aren't I? Silly me." I glanced up at the ceiling, feigning exasperation with myself.

I pulled a crumpled five-pound note out of my pocket. I then held it with both hands and pulled it straight a few times before laying it on the meeting table for all to see. They stared at the money.

"Jill, you are the company secretary. Aren't you? And you've got the share ledger right there?" I pointed at the book she'd just shown me. "Would you be so good as to fill in the details and issue me my five shares, please?"

She knew she had no alternative. It took what seemed like an eternity for her to complete the form. After checking the entries twice, I signed the register. She then tore out my certificate for five common shares in Dad's company.

"Thank you, Jill. Now, let's move on to the next item. The position of CEO. My father is no longer alive, and the position is vacant. I propose Roger Cockroft as CEO. All those in favor?" I had a quizzical look on my face. Then I rolled my eyes, again feigning realization at my own foolishness. "Oh, what am I thinking? I'm in favor, so the motion is carried unanimously."

They all looked stunned and dumbstruck, but I wasn't done yet. "Jill, thank you for your service, but you can step down from any and all responsibilities regarding the company. James, the same applies to you. You both have no board responsibilities. Do you understand?" Both nodded. Jill looked boiling. James just looked shocked.

"I will appoint Kim, my brother's wife, as company secretary. Absolutely everything has to be approved by her. You have no authority to spend a single penny." My demeanor had changed. I had their full attention.

"Now, are you going to tell me who fucking wants to buy my company?" Thunder was in my voice. My words struck like lightning.

Jack, the commercial director and third rebel, finally broke his silence and replied lamely, "I wish I'd known this was going to happen."

"I bet you did."

I ended the meeting. They'd been exposed for who they truly were: People my dad had once admired, trusted, and helped, who then proceeded to ruin his company and steal all his assets for their own gain. The situation was no longer salvageable. But thanks to my family's tenacity, we were able to pay off the bank, settle our debts, and make Mum secure. Dad would have liked that.

On the last day, before the factory closed its doors for good, I spoke to Alan, one of the machine operators. He had worked there for fifteen years, so I expected the worst.

"Roger, your dad was amazing. We all admired him. Did you know he had a rule about ice creams in the summer? He'd buy everyone ice creams, but only if it got so hot that he had to take his tie off."

He paused for a moment, gazing into space, remembering his last strawberry Mivvi. Then he looked up at me and finished, "I saw what those three were doing. We all did. You had no choice but to do this. It was the right thing."

With Dad's affairs finally settled, I returned my focus to my career, which just kept going up and up. I joined the accounting organization KPMG and set up a consulting practice where I'd jump into companies that had lost control, especially automotive supply companies. I served as the fixer. I'd take the reins and wrestle the crisis back under control. That type of clean-up work made me famous. The BBC, the *Financial Times*, and all the national newspapers wanted to know how I did it.

Rivals PricewaterhouseCoopers snatched me up, offering me even more money. My clients got bigger and bigger until I was leading assignments with major organizations, including JPMorgan Chase & Co. and oil giant BP. For about seven years I worked internationally, traveling all over Europe, Australia, New Zealand, the US, and Asia. I was always in demand because I had one skill everyone wanted: thriving when chaos ensues. I specialized in trouble and didn't panic under pressure. Panic never delivered the required results. In my mind, emotions functioned as enemies of order. Amid chaos, only calm and reason served as beacons of hope—a gift from my childhood.

My private life looked all but perfect too. From the outside, people would see I had a beautiful wife and three adorable children: Victoria, Benjamin, and Hugo. I had a country cottage in a wonderfully quaint village called Clayworth, a faithful dog, a Porsche, and a Land Rover. Locals called me Captain Cash. Love formed the foundation of our family despite Charlotte's waning carnal interest. Yes, everything appeared perfect. But not for me. Deep down, I felt I could do better.

Then I got a call in 2003 from someone who had been a client of mine. She wanted me to go work in America—specifically in Baltimore, Maryland—where I would be one of the top executives at Constellation Energy, a multi-billion-dollar company. It sounded to me like a great job and perhaps a chance to fix the tiny cracks in my marriage. I'd commute to Baltimore, but our new hometown would be Annapolis with a mansion nestled on the shores of the bay—a new life, a new start.

Constellation Energy did all things related to power: commodity trading, retail sales, power generation, and even ownership of America's oldest utility company. Yet I would be responsible for changing everything—every process, every procedure, every system—so the company could grow even bigger. That's what I wanted to do: make something as good as it could be, on this scale, in this country.

The knives came out from day one. I was barging into well-guarded territory, the very culture of the firm. But I figured I would have to make some enemies in order to achieve the larger goal of greater profit. It was why I'd been hired. My boss was on her ascent. She wanted to make the company more efficient and didn't care about territorial battles. She had her sights set on growing the business and her career—all the way to the top. She appreciated that I moved with critical speed. I wasn't very diplomatic, but I kept her happy. It kept my job and my family safe.

Her opponents were equally powerful. As I stepped on their toes, I made more enemies. They had no room for the corporate police, and especially not an Englishman they saw as a spy. Suddenly, my boss was deposed when she faltered in a power struggle. I was the first sacrifice, locked into my office as a symbol of their victory. The lion had been caged.

Whatever I tried, I couldn't escape what they had already decided for me. I worked every angle I could think of, constantly proposing new ideas. But each time, I was returned to my cage. An exhibit, I served as a warning to anyone who challenged the status quo.

I'd created my own worst nightmare. I had to provide for my family, but I couldn't settle for a window job, a humdrum existence for the rest of my career, looking out my office window or over my shoulder every day, just trying to survive.

No, I wasn't finished trying. I had to fix this.

PART 1

MELTING POT

CHAPTER 2

Heaven's Haven

NOVEMBER 9, 2007
FARSUND, NORWAY

Stein Ytterdahl looked out from his kitchen window over the archipelago, past the islands, and south, into the North Sea. The sun had not yet risen, but a deep red aurora caught the underside of the highest clouds. Still in pajamas, he cradled his warm coffee. Ytterdahl was a strong man, not tall but sturdy. In his early fifties, he had a full head of gray hair, matching sideburns, and a well-trimmed goatee. He dedicated all his time to his new job as mayor of Farsund, his hometown. And today would be his opportunity to shine. Farsund would bloom again if the pipe-maker came back into town.

The "pipe-maker" referred to Bredero Shaw, a company that made gas pipelines to install at the bottom of the sea. They did this all over the world, and Farsund had been one of their most important manufacturing hubs. Their last project, which produced 750 miles of pipeline, had boosted the city's fortunes tremendously over just five years. The process yielded one million tons of huge, 3.5-foot diameter pipes, coated in concrete. Almost seven hundred massive container ships had been loaded with the finished product. Eventually, the pipes connected one of the biggest natural gas fields in northern Norway to the UK, supplying 25 percent of the gas the country consumed each year.

But when the project ended in March 2006, the Farsund site lay idle. The factory was mothballed, and the docks sat empty. Everyone who worked there lost their jobs. The community became a deserted ghost town as people moved away and shops closed. What had once boomed now went bust.

Today, though, the "pipe-maker" would finally get confirmation of whether it had won a much larger project, twice the size of the previous one. This project would stretch across Russia: Nord Stream 1. They had already chosen Farsund as their production site. The project would keep the community busy for the next five years. Prosperity would flow once again.

Ytterdahl cared deeply for this community where his family had lived for so long. Naturally they'd been delighted by his election, which he won on the promise of bringing security and happiness back to Farsund. He knew how different Farsund was from other towns in this region. Most served the oil industry directly, so men and women worked offshore for weeks on end, leaving their families behind to travel to oil platforms or to board survey ships. Farsund, meanwhile, had jobs at home. And it wasn't just Bredero Shaw that offered hundreds of local jobs. The metal-maker and the car parts factory (Bil-Fabrikken) provided still more. Ytterdahl was well-aware that if all three big employers did well, they would support the entire community. This meant families could stay together, play together, and, most importantly, live together.

Ytterdahl quickly finished his coffee and scuttled off to get ready for the day. He donned his most professional business suit. The local press, the Farsund Avis, *would surely photograph him today.*

As he walked down the road to his office, he passed by scores of small islands dotting the waters around him. These islands served as reminders of how wedded Farsund's centuries-long history was to the sea and to trade—that is, illegal trade. Farsund had once been a pirate town. During the 1600s and 1700s, the town's residents plundered the surrounding seas, through which a bountiful trade route passed. Back then it became the basis of the town's economic survival. Pirates would dart out from behind those tiny islands and grab whatever passed, feeding off the rich cargo bound for Russia. Then, usually chased by the British Navy, they'd duck back into the myriad of channels, confusing their pursuers. Only they knew which routes to take. Only they knew where the rocks lay, just beneath the water's surface. Their knowledge led them to rich rewards and their pursuers to peril.

But when the Napoleonic War erupted in 1803, piracy became essential, and the King of Norway and Denmark sanctioned its legitimacy. It became brutal. The locals had to confront the sheer might of Her Majesty's Royal Navy, bent on annihilating any who did not conform to Britain's authority and dominance. The fight raged on for a decade, burdening Farsund with significant poverty and hardship. Massively outgunned and short on resources, the buccaneers could only draw on intellect,

agility, and bravery to protect their fragile community from
a formidable foe.

Over time, piracy ebbed, but the sense of trade never died.
By the late nineteenth century, trade and transporting cargo,
which involved skilled seamanship, became the backbone
of the town. Anyone looking for a seasoned captain and
professional crew need look no further than Farsund. Two
prominent families, Lund and Brinch, built a large fleet of
ships, all managed from the town's harbor and regarded with
great respect. That became the key: Reputation was essential
if the town was to grow. And reputation depended on each
individual person who lived there. Do something right, and
your actions stayed with you and your descendants forever.
Everyone did their part to uphold this mantra. Because over
the decades, the town gathered pace and grew to a population
of three thousand with another seven thousand in surrounding
villages. All were combined under what became known as the
"Farsund Kommune."

In the center of Farsund, Ytterdahl walked past a cluster of
small white cottages crammed together on the water's edge.
He ambled down another block of grand offices, which once
housed fleet commanders and then finally glimpsed the
Kommune offices before him—but first, a detour to the local
bakery. He dipped inside and was instantly greeted by the
smell of freshly baked bread.

"Good morning, Margret! Can I take a bolle, please?"

Before Margret had a chance to answer, Ytterdahl reached over
the counter and grabbed a delicious, still-warm bun peppered

with raisins—the perfect match for his second cup of coffee. Leaving ten kroner on the counter, he now headed straight to his office with a smile on his face. Today was going to be a good day. He was sure of it.

Grethe Hindersland, the general manager of the car parts factory, had already been at work for two hours. Hers wasn't an easy job—but then, she never liked easy. A graduate engineer, she had worked her way up the ranks of Alcoa, one of the largest metal-making operations in the world transforming special rocks into glowing aluminum. Grethe was as tough as the machines used in that powerful process. She could face any challenge head-on, and she expected the same from those below her.

At thirty-six, she was one of the youngest general managers ever, leading one of the most sophisticated plants in Alcoa's arsenal. Her team was responsible for manufacturing unique aluminum parts, all destined for automotive giants like Volvo, Saab, BMW, and even Ferrari. Each part was cast in a custom mold, unique to the exact requirements of each customer.

Grethe was readying herself for a tour of the factory, something she did every morning. She reasoned it would always be better to see a problem with her own eyes than to hear about it later. She did one last check of her well-worn company uniform: dark-blue workwear trousers and jacket; heavy metal toe-capped boots; a red hard hat over her mouse-brown hair; safety glasses; and thick gloves. The entire outfit made her feel strong and prepared for anything.

Today, though, as she strode down the corridor between the offices and the factory, Grethe was uncharacteristically distracted. She had been on calls with the head office in Pittsburg. It hadn't gone well. She knew Alcoa had been intending to get rid of the car parts factory. Now she'd been told the deal was done. A private equity firm had bought it. She had no idea what a private equity firm was. She only knew they were based in New York. A flurry of questions shot through her mind. She was a factory manager, not a CEO. She didn't know how to run a company. She only knew how to make machines work.

And now those complex machines loomed in front of her as the factory doors opened automatically: cranes, conveyors, robots, and mammoth casting machines, all stretching across three hundred thousand square feet; all furiously busy. Each casting machine spat out four large cast parts for every cycle. Instantly, a robot would grab the newly formed parts and whisk them away on special frames eighty feet above the floor and then drop them down briefly to the next step in the convoluted production process. There, different robots would compete for each part. Their arms intertwined but never crashed into each other. Parts were automatically machined or inspected by X-ray and then sent on to the next step. The hive of automated bustle nearly hid the human factor, but dotted here and there were the experts. They were the ones controlling this delicate and extremely technical process. Highly trained, they had the foresight to spot a problem before it happened.

Grethe always started her inspection at the beginning of the process. She walked down a series of marked walkways until she reached the three receiving furnaces at the other end of the factory. The furnaces resembled giant pots with special lids fixed firmly in place. The massive metal reservoirs could hold tons of this lethal white-hot liquid. A wild, corrosive beast—contained.

Grethe watched the first delivery of the day from behind the safety screen. As the bright glowing liquid poured into the furnace, her mind wandered back to the call from her boss. Now Alcoa had decided to distance itself from making car parts, so who were these new owners? Did they know how important the metal-maker and the car parts factory were to Farsund? Did they know each depended on the other to survive? She had to have hot liquid metal to make her manufacturing process work. They had no other way of melting ingots (solid metal) into liquid. Without one company, the other couldn't survive.

"Okay, I see… But isn't there anything I can do? I could talk to them perhaps. No? Okay, I understand. It's just that this is so…"

It was late, and a fierce winter storm raged outside, lashing the waves in the harbor. Ytterdahl had spent the entire day in his office on the phone, but his focus remained six hundred miles away, in the office of his caller—the head of Norwegian operations for Bredero Shaw, the pipe-maker. He listened to every word, trying to interpret his caller's intonations and sighs. The news wasn't good.

"I just don't understand why the Russians decided to pick that company. Bredero Shaw are clearly the best. You guys are the world leaders," Ytterdahl continued.

His voice grew more desperate. "Are there any other contracts you could move to Farsund? I'll do all I can to make it easy for you. No? Okay, I see. Well, call me anytime if things change. Yes, yes. Good night."

Ytterdahl had never felt more dejected. He picked up his cup and took a swig but quickly spat it out. The coffee had lost its heat long ago. He flopped back into his chair, looked up at the ceiling, and then screamed, "Fuck!"

Farsund just lost three hundred jobs.

Set Sails

NOVEMBER 9, 2007
LAS VEGAS, NEVADA

The British frigate honed into view, sails unfurled and full of wind. She was on a mission, intent on one thing: to sink the ship that lay dead ahead and drown every last pirate. With a flagrant command from her captain, all forward facing cannons lit up. Then a deafening cacophony of explosions befell the pirate ship. The gun powder room had been hit.

Despite the chaos, the buccaneer didn't surrender. He swung from the aft of his crippled vessel to the bow using a rope dangling from the main mast. A red bandana kept his hair in order, and a dashing hat held everything firmly in place. His boots looked like true pirate boots too—knee-high leather and cuffed at the top. Heroic music and a pre-recorded speech began playing on the PA system. It sounded tenacious and optimistic. The crowd crammed together on the sidewalk outside Treasure Island, enthralled. How would this end?

I was on the fifteenth floor of the Treasure Island Hotel. My room faced the oversized pond where the two mechanical ships battled every hour, on the hour. It was hard not to hear the booming cannons, the loud music, and the buccaneer's persistent screams.

But I had other things to consider. I would be the opening keynote speaker for an international conference on business process excellence, housed in the much grander Venetian Hotel. I would have liked to stay there, but my hotel was cheaper. The sound of the cannon fire reminded me why.

That evening, I lay in bed rehearsing my speech, thinking about my past. I'd chosen seven stories to highlight seven key lessons I'd learned throughout my career. Each scenario was vastly different, ranging from goliath steel-making plants in Europe and oil refineries in Asia to investment banks in London. They had all been clients at some point. As a professional fixer, it was my job to make them better; to make things work. I'd go in, find what was broken, and why it broke. The deeper I went, the better the fix.

Today, however, I was fixing a different type of problem—my own. I was out of a job although technically still a corporate vice president from a Fortune 500 company—at least for a few more weeks. They'd been generous when they killed me, offering me a reasonable package and telling me I could keep my title until the end of November, just enough time to do one last conference.

My chance to meet a new employer finally came. The alarm on my phone was pointless. I'd been awake most of the night. I spent longer than usual making sure I looked as professional as possible: clean white shirt, dark blue suit, overly polished shoes. I packed a computer and copious notes into my distressed briefcase, double-checked it, and then took one last look in the mirror to see if I looked okay. I didn't.

The elevator sped me to the ground floor, straight into the center of the casino. Punters were still feeding money into slot machines, others transfixed on the cards in front of them. They'd been here all night, desperate for a win. Meanwhile, I was praying for something even more unlikely: a win to change my life.

The conference room wasn't a room. It was a massive hall, hidden in the Venetian Hotel's maze of floors where halls like these could easily house hundreds, even thousands, of people. Five hundred chairs had been laid out, split by a large central corridor. Three screens loomed at the far end, dwarfing the size of a football field.

I arrived early, but the technicians were already expecting me. My presentation was projected on all three screens. They had set up a huge control platform with hundreds of dials and knobs, all with a specific purpose only they knew. Quickly, a technician wired me up with a mic attached to my shirt. Then the testing began. They asked me to talk.

"What do you want me to say?" I was slightly intimidated by the AV guy next to me. My voice reverberated around the room.

"Just tell me what you had for breakfast," he replied.

"Eh, um! I didn't have anything yet," I boomed. "Where do I have to go to get coffee?"

I got a thumbs up from the control booth. I was all set.

The conference started at 8:00 a.m. sharp, and every seat was taken. After welcoming the audience, the host introduced me as the corporate VP of my soon-to-be ex-company. I stood up, hesitated a moment, looked at my introduction slide, paused, and then gazed out at the sea of faces staring back at me. I felt sick, and my mouth was dry. This was my last chance.

I sucked in my fear and launched into my speech. Things got better. I was surprised by how smoothly everything went: the vignettes, the pace, the tone. I had reached the last slide before I knew it. Solid applause greeted my last words, and a slew of questions followed.

I felt like the star of the show. At the first break, everyone wanted to talk to me. This was just what I needed—a whole load of new contacts. They asked for my business card, which was a problem because it was about to expire. I told them my supply had run out but made sure I grabbed theirs. I gathered as many as I could. I would contact all of them after the conference. Maybe someone out there needed someone like me.

The crowd began thinning as the day wound down. Just when I was losing hope, a man approached me. He had jet-black hair and a face that looked as though it had been stretched across his chubby cheeks, so much that his eyes squinted. He spoke with a thick Kentucky accent.

"Hi, my name's Kyle, Kyle Crammer. I heard you today. I liked what you said."

I'd never met him before, but we'd both worked for Toyota, which made us connected. Now he was in private equity, working for some firm based out of New York. They'd just bought a company in Norway.

"Norway is a problem," he said with his Southern drawl. "They don't have one single clue how to run a company. I need someone to be out there full time."

My heart beat a little faster, but I tried to look nonchalant.

"It's just a pity I can't get someone like you. But you've got a job. Don't you?" His face looked down but his eyes kept contact with mine. He was egging me on.

I bit. "Ah, well, it's funny you say that. I actually have just set up my own business as an independent consultant. This is sort of in my wheelhouse." I didn't want to sound too eager.

"How much do you cost?" The real question.

I'll screw this up if I ask for too much, but I don't want to leave anything on the table.

"How about twenty-five hundred dollars per day?" I figured he'd knock me down. I'd accept less, much less.

"Deal. Can you do three months?"

Everything flashed through my mind. I would set up a business to do exactly this (like the one I just claimed to already have). I'd build my reputation if I did this job well—with a New York private equity firm. And I could do Norway. I'd been to Oslo a few times. It wasn't so bad. A long way away but not so bad.

I tried to steady my voice, to make it sound like I was still debating. "And when would you want me to be out there?"

"I need you there next week. Can you get there by the fourteenth?" He already assumed I would do the job. He was right.

"Um, I think I can make that work." I had a thoughtful expression on my face. "Let me take a look." I pulled out my Blackberry and opened my calendar. I had nothing in there at all. Completely empty.

"Yes, yes, I can do that."

We continued talking for some minutes more, exchanging details. Then I asked, "Tell me, Kyle, why me? Is it because of what I said today?"

"Kind of. But mostly because we need someone who doesn't care about working over Thanksgiving. All my guys want to go home, but you're a Brit. You don't care."

He was right again. I didn't. All that mattered was I'd just scored my first gig as a free agent.

A new spring was in my step as I headed back to my hotel with a solution that quashed both my fears. I could provide for my family, and I could also keep bettering myself.

The pirate show was in full swing again. With no way to pass through the crowd, I decided to watch the finishing scene. Once again, the intrepid pirate energetically swung from his rope, across the full length of his vessel. Nothing worked on his ship—save one cannon, loaded and aimed directly at the British frigate. He lit the fuse and fired. The cannon ball found its mark.

As the crowd dispersed, I lingered. The pirate used everything he had available. He never gave up and never showed fear, even when dangling from a rope with the odds stacked against him. Perhaps this was my lesson from Las Vegas after all.

CHAPTER 4

The Transition

NOVEMBER TO DECEMBER 2007

"Look at the wonderful scene, Benj. The most precious moments are priceless and free."

My son, Benjamin, sat by my side. We were watching the sun set over the turquoise sea. I was trying to tell him to look for the good in change. I knew our lives were about to transform very soon.

Then someone else chimed in. "Asshole!" a driver screamed to the clueless pedestrian who had decided to meander across the street, directly in front of his convertible. He was loud enough to be heard over his screeching tires; loud enough to grab our attention as we sat on the fourth-floor balcony of a tired-looking, puce-pink hotel. We both burst out laughing.

Ben had just turned eleven. This was the final day of his birthday present, a three-day trip to Key West. He'd learned to scuba dive and graduated from his course, so we were celebrating with pizza on that balcony. We enjoyed every last minute and just wished we could stretch out our time together. But the day was coming to an end, and tomorrow was going to be busy.

"Will we do more of this, Daddy? Will we come back here again? A boys' trip?" He was fishing. His eyes were the bait. All he wanted was time with his dad.

Early the next morning, we flew back to Maryland. My timing was impeccable at the airport, because I'd practiced this many times before. I quickly seized our luggage from the carousel and then hauled it to the international departure hall. Charlotte and my two other children, Victoria and Hugo, were waiting there. They stood next to the check-in desk with a big gray suitcase, my fresh luggage in exchange for this spent bag.

The second my two other kids caught sight of me, they ran and jumped into my arms, screaming, "Daddy!" Their voices echoed through the giant, high-ceilinged hall. I hugged them so hard. Charlotte joined in. She wrapped her arms around me, and we kissed passionately.

But the happiness on her face suddenly dissolved into concern. An announcement had just been made over the loudspeaker. They were calling all passengers to check in. This was my next flight.

We continued hugging each other, an island of intertwined arms. Charlotte had already told Victoria and Hugo that I was leaving. Talking to Benj was my job. I hadn't done it yet.

He was shocked I was getting on another plane so shortly after the last one.

"Where are you going, Daddy? How long will you be gone?"

And the most difficult question of all. "Why, Daddy? Why?"

Charlotte now stood on the verge of tears. She locked eyes with me and whispered, "You will come back. Won't you?"

We both knew this was a node. A critical point. An unknown path stretched ahead of me. But I was determined to take it. I knew the reward. It allowed me to provide for everyone. To make them safe.

I cupped her face. "You are my life."

A check-in counter assistant interrupted our goodbye. "You'll need to check your luggage if you want it on the plane."

It was time to go. I dropped my suitcase and hugged them all one last time. "I'll be back at Christmas. I love you," I whispered to Charlotte.

As I walked away, I looked over my shoulder. Charlotte mopped back tears. Victoria clutched Hugo and Benjamin. All three of their faces asked the same thing: "Why, Daddy? Why?"

I held everything in and cleared security.

I didn't sleep well on the first plane to Heathrow, and I didn't sleep at all on the second plane to Copenhagen. By the time I boarded the third, I could have slept standing up. But it was the shortest flight of my life. I sat down and closed my eyes before we took off. Next thing I knew, we were taxiing on the dinky runway of Kristiansand Airport in Norway.

Freezing rain and strong winds slapped me sharply in the face as I stepped out of the plane. I descended the narrow stairs as quickly as possible and headed to the luggage conveyer. Luckily, I spied my huge gray suitcase already making the rounds. I hauled it off the belt onto the floor. This hulking beast would take me through the next six weeks.

Finally, I found the car rental desk. I'd chosen the cheapest and smallest rental car available, a Toyota Aygo. After dropping the passenger and back seats down, I managed to squeeze all my belongings inside. I was ready for the first part of my adventure: finding Farsund.

I managed to locate the main road through the center of Kristiansand. In the last light of the day, I could make out the ominous silhouette of storm clouds rolling in. Commuters crowded the highway, hurrying to get home ahead of this storm. But traffic ground to a halt once I reached one of the many tunnels passing under the city center. The air in the tunnel was cloudy and full of dust from salt spread to melt any snow that might fall. The salt had collected in the tunnels and made it difficult to see or breathe.

Once I exited the tunnel, I got my first true glimpse of Norwegian beauty. The road to Farsund took me past the main ferry terminal in Kristiansand, where a huge catamaran was swallowing up hundreds of cars bound for Denmark. Twinkles of light seemed sandwiched between the sea below and the storm clouds above. They lit the underside of the clouds, revealing every swirl and shadow. Since the islands dotting the sea made Kristiansand a difficult port to navigate, a series of red and green lights flashed to help sailors pick out safe routes. This was a rugged land, where nature coexisted with industry and where you had to be tough to survive.

The last few rays of light disappeared. I drove into an ink-black void. Norway reserves a special kind of darkness for the nights before the first snow of winter arrives. The ground seems to swallow up every molecule of light. I inched my way slowly along the main E39 road. Though this road connected Kristiansand and Stavanger, two major cities, in some places it was less than two lanes wide. Not fun in the dark. Then rain erupted. To make matters worse, none of the road names or towns I passed matched those on my route instructions. And every time I tried to sneak a peek at the map on my lap, I would look up to find I had drifted into oncoming traffic and needed to wrestle my car from impending disaster.

I estimated it would take ninety minutes to get to Farsund. The time ticked past, and ninety minutes came and went. I was lost. Had I missed the turn? As I debated whether to go back, I suddenly spied the sign to Farsund. I turned off the highway and headed through the small town of Lyngdal, picking my way along a winding road skirting a fjord. The road had been rutted by so many years of use that water was collecting in the tire tracks and causing my car to aquaplane. My wipers were working full-speed, but I still struggled to see through the torrential downpour. If I made one small mistake, I'd plummet straight down the side of a mountain and into the icy black waters of the fjord below.

I managed to reach Farsund but was still horribly lost. I had driven out, back, and through the tortuous roads five or six times. Desperate, I called Charlotte and asked her to look on the internet for directions to the Rederiet Hotell.

As Charlotte searched for a map to guide me, I had to take another call ringing on my phone. It was Stanley Cuttle, a representative of the private equity firm who'd hired me. He was on site and waiting, clearly disgruntled I hadn't arrived earlier. I could detect his frustration through the phone. He wanted to finish up at the factory and have his dinner.

"Well, Roger," he said with a Kentucky accent. He drew out the first letter of my name, so it sounded like "Rrrrrroger." Like the trilling warning of a rattlesnake. "Just meet me for dinner as fast as you damn well can."

The call ended, and I suddenly noticed the very obvious sign facing me on the side of the hill. The Rederiet Hotell was right in front of me. Somehow I had missed it.

Dating from the 1930s, the hotel sits atop a fifty-foot granite rock and looks out over the fjords and into the North Sea. The building had once held the offices of a shipping company, and in many ways it still looked and smelled like an office. The receptionist welcomed me in Norwegian, and I tried to explain who I was in rudimentary English. I spoke very slowly, trying to make myself as easy to understand as possible. "My name Roger Cockroft… I have room here." The inflection in my voice rose at the end of the last word, so it sounded more like a question than a statement—a question I hoped would be answered in the affirmative.

In perfect English, she replied, "Ah, Mr. Cockroft! I've booked you in for the next six weeks. Is that right?" Red-faced, I confirmed my stay, checked in, and scuttled off to my room, dumped my stuff, and, following the receptionist's directions, headed out to meet my new employer.

The New York private equity firm was colloquially referred to as the "Money Men." They were on a wild spending spree across the globe and had picked up everything they could. They'd bought a US factory from Alcoa, the global aluminum producer, and had been persuaded to take on this plant in Norway too. They'd essentially gotten a two-for-one deal because the Norway operation wasn't making any money. If they could make the Farsund plant profitable quickly, they'd keep it. Otherwise, they were going to let it close. They didn't care, as long as they didn't lose any money.

I'd met Kentucky Kyle in Vegas. He was the one who'd offered me this job. Now I was about to meet his prodigy, Stanley Cuttle. The Money Men wanted me to cut as much cost as possible. Stanley Cuttle just wanted to get back home. But not before he made it clear he was in charge and I was the hired help.

He was waiting at the only other hotel in town, the Farsund Fjordhotel.

"Well, look who finally turned up." His drawn-out accent didn't mask his impatience. He stuffed his mouth with a forkful of boiled potatoes.

Cuttle told me how he thought the company could become more efficient. His words conveyed the enthusiastic naivete of someone who has never had to live with the aftermath of what "efficiency" really means. While he pontificated about improving certain processes and reducing scrap, he never mentioned how many people had to lose their jobs before this company turned a profit. He finished talking after an hour of hot air.

Finally it was time to get some sleep. But Norway had one last wake-up call waiting for me as I stepped out into the parking lot. What people in Farsund call "a little storm" slammed into me hard. The gale blew down from the north and across the fjords with a deafening roar. I felt as if I were standing in a wind tunnel with someone training a fire hose straight at me. I was soaking wet before I reached my car.

The hotel room wasn't welcoming. I listened to the storm booming outside and rattling my bedroom window panes. I shivered on my slab-like bed with the ratty comforter pulled tightly up to my nose. In the gloom of the twenty-five-watt light bulb, I closed my eyes and thought, *Oh god, what have I done?* I was thirty-five hundred miles from home and in some sort of pissing contest with Stanley in a country where I couldn't even read let alone pronounce the street names. I drifted into a fitful sleep.

Morning came. I drew back my curtains and was greeted by a stunning sight. The sun was just starting to rise into a deep-blue crystal-clear sky. Everything appeared freshly washed. Glistening raindrops clung to railings, windowsills, and tree branches, catching the morning sun and glinting like diamonds. I showered and got dressed quickly so I could go for a walk through town.

Farsund is built on the side of a steep granite hill and surrounded by an impressive fjord to the south and towering mountains to the north. Although it's not quite an island, it has the look and feel of one. You reach it by two bridges, and it's almost entirely surrounded by water. The shops and offices sit at the bottom of the hill toward the harbor in the center of town. As you climb the steep hill, the town's shops give way to homes, each one boasting a breathtaking view over the southern archipelago of Norway.

The hotel where I was staying was near the waterfront amid all the shops, including the bakery Larsen, which had its door open wide. The smell of newly baked buns and bread, mixed with the aroma of freshly brewed coffee, drew me inside. I started talking to the ladies who ran the shop. They were all in their fifties and sixties. Each wore an apron and a warm, welcoming smile as they spoke to me, again in perfect English. They wanted to know if I was there on vacation or if I had come on business. Perhaps, they inquired, because of the *bilfabriken*, the car parts factory? They didn't miss a thing. This town was really very small.

I strolled to the harborside. Yesterday the sea had been ferocious, but this morning it was so calm and mirror-like it reflected the town's image perfectly. The harbor stretched the entire length of the town. Long planks of wood ran parallel to it with gaps between each one, just wide enough to lose a cell phone or a set of keys in the waters below. Fishing boats jostled for space with yachts moored along the quayside. The buildings facing the water looked as though they had once been grand but were now a little tired. All of them shared the same breathtaking views of the sea, mountains, and fjords. Yet the inhabitants didn't seem to notice the jewel afforded to them every day. Or perhaps they were too polite and humble to brag about it.

I finished the last bite of my bun and glanced at my watch. Time had slipped away without my noticing. I rushed back to the hotel, jumped into my shoebox car, and sped off to the factory.

My destination was situated about two miles out of town. I drove into the parking lot and got my first sight. It looked big and bland from the outside, with yellow doors and bright blue walls—just like IKEA, the Scandinavian standard. Inside evoked the same mood. Every chair and table appeared as if it had started life as a flatpack puzzle.

Grethe Hindersland, the factory manager, and Helge Fait, the human resource manager, greeted me at the reception. Cuttle was there too. Grethe made sure the factory operated properly, and Helge dealt with employee issues. They were "originals," meaning they'd been at the factory from the start. (I later discovered most people working there were "originals.") Grethe had a fighting spirit I liked instantly. Helge, a tall man with a neat gray beard and mustache, remained very quiet, preferring to just watch me and Stanley. He had learned to observe before he committed.

As we walked toward the machines, Stanley boasted, "Of course, this place is nothing like Toyota. We'd made that place just about as good as it could be before I left."

Grethe ignored him and began showing me the process of casting car parts in aluminum. Whenever I had a question, she would pause and consider the answer carefully before speaking. When she didn't know the answer, she was comfortable enough to admit it. Cuttle, on the other hand, just kept fuming and blustering. Nothing was right or good enough. No area was clean enough. "Things are going to change," he repeated over and over. "Shape up or ship out." He proved to be a typical empty can. They make the most noise.

Plenty of robots were doing the hard work. The level of automation gave the factory floor an eerie feel of emptiness. Though well-lit, it was very hard to spot any of the workers as they went about their daily tasks in between the huge machines and busy robots. Every so often, a huge blast of compressed air signified a team was working on the daily maintenance for one of the tools. Occasionally I would see a maintenance technician hurtling off to deal with a minor repair on one of the many tricycles they used to transport their toolboxes. Other than that, it was easy to imagine myself walking alone around the factory. In fact, there were sixty sets of eyes on each of the three daily shifts, scattered around the factory floor, working tirelessly to make the giant casting machines pump out thousands of parts every day. They didn't miss a beat and saw everything.

Sure, the plant could improve, but it was obvious that considerable thought had gone into making this a truly impressive operation. The technology and automation were mind-blowing. I'd had the advantage of working across many businesses around the world. I already put this plant in the top one percent of what I'd seen. Engineering and efficiency weren't the problem.

The problem was too many of the casting machines stood idle. There were simply not enough orders to keep all the machines busy. Most had been switched off. Why had this factory been abandoned? It used to be a show piece in Alcoa's fleet. Then they'd shifted their strategy, going upstream to make more metal and fewer parts. The factory's new owners, the Money Men, needed to find a way of getting new orders. That wasn't my focus.

I spent the next six weeks trying to make the factory even more efficient. It was what Kentucky Kyle wanted. I'd snip away at unnecessary process steps and eliminate bottlenecks. I delved into all the details. Some people didn't like the new owner, so they quit. I didn't replace them, but I also didn't fire anyone. Meanwhile, Cuttle was no help at all. His prime goal was to make sure everything looked good when Kentucky Kyle visited. Most of the time he wasn't even at the factory.

During those six weeks, I often asked myself if anything I'd been tasked to do would make the slightest difference. *What do I care? I'm only here until March*, I would think. But I knew that wasn't true.

I decided to take a walk around town the night before Christmas Eve. One last look before I flew home. It was cold, and the moon shone brightly. Every surface was coated in an inch of the most beautiful thick frost, which caught the gleam of moonlight and made everything appear silver. I crunched my way through the frost into the heart of town. Families were already celebrating. Log fires roared inside their cozy white houses. Children played with new toys, and parents beamed with happiness. Decorations glittered and reflected a multitude of colors. I smelled the heady scent of home-cooked food, a glorious combination of ginger, cinnamon, sugar, and mulled wine. I so wanted to knock on a door and invite myself in.

But I wasn't part of that community. I was still an outsider. I could only observe it longingly through those icy windows. This was a magical place—so fragile, so delicate, so precious. I felt privileged to be there.

CHAPTER 5

The Observation Period

___

JANUARY 2008

White-hot aluminum can do terrible things. At over fourteen hundred degrees Fahrenheit, it tries to eat through anything it touches. If it encounters water, a severe chemical reaction will ensue, splitting out the hydrogen and exploding like a bomb. Every single moment aluminum tests its containment, looking for the slightest cracks, the tiniest faults. It seems to want nothing more than to create absolute and total devastation as payback for being confined. The only way to prevent ruin is to be equally determined and equally alert.

___

Helge burst into the office. He stretched his hands wide and held them out in front of him, grasping the air. With a look of desperation on his face, he tried to think of the right English word. Then he yelled, "Crisis!"

Crisis would do.

Suddenly all the alarms shrilled in unison. Grethe left us and darted straight toward the factory. Everyone else followed Helge and the rest of the office staff into the parking lot. Outside the nastily cold air stung our cheeks. Wrapped in our coats, we milled around in front of the main entrance, trying to find out what had happened. Bob Baker, one of the Money Men, was there. The consummate professional, he never seemed to lose his cool. He would always assess a situation in the simplest terms, saying either, "That's a good thing," or "That's a bad thing." When we heard the news there had been a metal spill, Bob said, "That's a bad thing," with a smile on his face.

Thirty minutes passed and we still didn't fully know the extent of the damage, only that it took precedence over our interrupted meeting. Bob and I huddled in the parking lot chatting and trying to stay warm. Suddenly, fire trucks screamed past to the back of the factory. Grethe returned and began talking with the operations staff. Then I saw a young man on a tricycle, pedaling furiously around the outside of the building.

He skidded the back wheels to a full stop and jumped off the trike. He was short and slim and wimpy looking. A red helmet partially covered his straw-like hair. He looked sweaty and flustered, with white soot dusting his face and uniform. He rushed over to Grethe to explain what had happened. Everyone nearby began surrounding the young man, patting him on the back with looks of awe and gratitude.

Grethe walked over to me and Bob. "The factory was in serious danger of exploding. That kid, Geir, saved it," she said as she pointed to the sweaty maintenance tech. By now an entire team of people encircled the boy, congratulating him.

I was shocked. I didn't know the factory could blow up. All I could think of asking was, "What happened?"

"There was a breakout in the number two receiving furnace," Grethe said. "Somehow the metal ate through the sidewall, and about two tons leaked onto the floor and into the drainage channels. That young man found a way of stopping the leak and isolating the furnace before he turned it off."

"What? He just turned it off?" I still couldn't comprehend what he had done.

"No. It wasn't that easy. He had to work exactly where the metal was leaking out. A puddle was between his feet. He had to dam the canal that connects the furnace to the casting machines. He literally poured porcelain blocks into the canal. They splashed molten metal onto his jacket."

She could tell I still didn't get it, so she continued to explain what must've been obvious to everyone else. "If he hadn't, power would be cut and the whole canal would turn into a 260-foot-long lump of metal. All our best casting machines would be wrecked.

"We've lost that furnace. It could have been much worse. At least we've still got the machines. All that metal on the floor—it could have burnt him alive. If it had found water… Boom." She made a movement with her hands to emphasize her words. "No more factory. No more Geir."

I wanted to see the disaster for myself. Stupidly, I asked Bob to accompany me to the spill despite being strongly advised not to. As we entered the deserted factory, I saw glowing metal filling every channel surrounding receiving furnace number two. Though it had a silvery skin indicating it had cooled down a bit, it still glowed orange underneath.

I looked at where Geir had risked his life. There on the floor were the remains of the sole from one of his boots. Surrounded by metal, it had melted into a barely recognizable black blob. Just a small bit of tread remained, a sight which terrified me. It drove home how lethal liquid metal truly was and how fearlessly Geir had acted in order to save the factory.

Later that day at the hotel bar, I recounted the story to Rainier, the hotel manager. When I finished I still felt perplexed. "I just don't get why he was so bold. He could have been vaporized or, worse, burnt to death. It's only a factory. It's not worth dying for."

Polishing a glass with his bar cloth, Rainier casually replied, "This is Farsund. We know everyone. His friends work there and some of his family. They all know him. They'll certainly remember what he did."

He paused, leaned on the bar, and looked me straight in the eyes. "This is a small community. It's not like where you come from. People don't forget what you do here." He thought for a minute. He hadn't really explained what he wanted to tell me.

Then he chimed in, "My fiancée is the granddaughter of the sea captain. Do you understand what that means? Her grandfather was an upstanding leader in this community, but he's dead. He died fifteen years ago, yet she is still defined by his actions and reputation.

"Memories last a long time here. We remember people and what they did. We honor the brave in Farsund."

There, the penny dropped. I envied Geir. He had been challenged like never before, and he confronted the challenge without hesitation, regardless of personal sacrifice. He fought to protect what he valued. His courage proved his honesty, his sincerity, and his loyalty. He'd created a legacy that would be remembered for decades.

CHAPTER 6

Good Times

FEBRUARY 2008 TO AUGUST 2009

It was a Sunday afternoon in February, a few weeks after the metal spill. Grethe and I were in her office late, preparing budgets for the year. We'd both survived a difficult week. Kentucky Kyle had raged into town with his sidekick, Cuttle. The duo had howled out demands for cutting costs, and then they tried to sack a bunch of people. Their bullying tactics infuriated me because I knew their plan was way too simple. All they wanted to do was cut costs and, at the same time, ask our customers to pay more. We didn't need to piss off our customers. We needed new orders. Kentucky Kyle and Cuttle went to Ferrari and KTM. Ferrari said no to their demand to raise prices. KTM just canceled their order.

"Do you know why they sold us?" Grethe looked intent.

Why had Alcoa sold this factory, the company she'd worked for so long, to these ruthless Money Men?

"See here. Look." Fraught, she pointed to a cell on her spreadsheet. "Look at those numbers. They're dreadful. The Volvo numbers are dropping *a lot*. By this time next year, we will have lost them completely. They'll stop building the cars that use our parts. This plant was built to make those parts for them."

She was running the numbers in her head again. "Next month we'll have to turn off another three machines."

My eyes widened. "We've got seventeen casting machines, and we're just going to use five of them?" No company could survive when it used less than one out of every three machines. It wouldn't make enough money.

"We were their vanity project," she vented as she tried to maintain her composure. It was true: Alcoa wanted to show the world they could make the impossible happen. They'd invested hundreds of millions of dollars building a state-of-the-art casting facility. Coupled with some of the best engineers Norway had to offer, the factory proved Alcoa could make miracles.

The new Porsche Panamera HAT part was a perfect example. It was a completely new subframe concept, holding the entire back of a car together and cast in one piece. That made it lighter, stronger, and cheaper than any other alternative. The trouble was Porsche didn't want very many of them because they didn't make many cars. Alcoa tried to sell the concept to other customers, but it was still an experiment. The Panamera hadn't been launched, and they hadn't proved it worked.

That was the irony: The very part that helped Alcoa look good was now making it look bad. So either they filled the factory up with more traditional orders or lived with a loss-making business. Alcoa was burning money but had to honor a commitment to Porsche to keep the factory open.

They came up with another quick and easy idea. Grethe frowned as she said, "They figured they could just give the company away and stop losing money. The Porsche part goes with the sale. It isn't Alcoa's problem anymore."

Everything pointed to a steadily deteriorating situation. Grethe and I both sensed that, but she was looking for my reassurance.

"What happens to me when you go?" She knew my contract ended in March. Soon I would return home and she would be on her own.

She grew more and more distressed as she spoke. "I don't know anything about your world. I don't know how finance works with private equity people. I'm not a sales person either. I just know how to run this factory."

She thought for a moment. "Even that's changed. If something broke when Alcoa owned us, we'd just fix it. The money was always there. Corporate would let us buy what we needed. What happens if I have another breakdown, like that furnace? How do I get the money to fix it from these guys?"

I froze, not knowing exactly what to say to console her and not fully believing there was even a way out.

"Is Kentucky Kyle just going to shout at me all the time?" she asked in desperation. "They fly here on first class airplanes and then insist we turn off two of every three lights in our factory to save pennies." She looked furious. "This is way more than I want to deal with. I'm sorry, Roger, but I quit. I want to be with my family."

Her voice trailed off as her eyes filled with tears. This was her home, all she had. She had been under incredible pressure. She didn't want to be seen to fail.

I had to do her job. Bob Baker insisted I step in, at least until the Money Men found someone to do it permanently. It would only be a couple more months, six at most, away from home. I didn't want Grethe gone. She was amazing. But filling in for her would build my credibility with New York.

The next three months turned Farsund from winter to spring. It felt like the factory bloomed in tandem with the flora and fauna on the mountains. Grethe had left me a very professional and well-run factory. So I chased new orders and grew my relationships with customers around the world.

General Motors was one of our earliest successes. I'd managed to convince the US giant to place a huge order with Farsund. The news had already spread to the community. The headlines of the local paper read, "New business at the Car Parts Factory," then they quoted me saying, "Farsund needs big business, and apparently big business needs Farsund." It had taken almost all of spring, but the process was finally ready, and the first part was made. It physically existed. I picked it up when it cooled down. What I held was jobs, livelihoods, and families. This new business would support all of those things. This was Farsund's future.

GM wasn't our only win. Peugeot gave us new business, then Bentley, then BMW increased their orders within their fleet and their Mini brand. Each time a new contract was awarded I ran the numbers, and each time the factory's future got better and better until finally we started to turn a profit.

The good vibe spread throughout the workforce and into the community. It even reached the guys in New York. Kentucky Kyle claimed the win as his doing, but Bob Baker was more pragmatic and focused only on business. He wanted to prove to the bankers Farsund was a good investment, and he had a credible management team. So he told me it was time to showcase everything we'd done to the bankers in London.

I met Bob at the Hilton hotel at Heathrow Airport. Tim Lima, my finance director and close friend, was there too. We entered a tidy, warm-hued room containing a long table, on the far side of which the bankers, Alan McClaren and two others, already sat. It was the first time I'd met Alan, though I'd seen his type before: professional with a risk-averse attitude.

Tim and I launched into our presentation. It went well. We were wrapping up after an hour. "…And if you look at our income here," Tim said as he pointed to the projection of his spreadsheet on the wall screen, "you can see we turn to strong profits early next year."

Then I stepped in. "Thanks, Tim. Gentlemen, we are winning new business, and our order book is looking strong. Very strong. Our future looks bright. Questions?"

Alan was impressed—so impressed he lent us more money. Tim and I were killing his risk, and we made him look good. That was important.

When the bankers left the meeting room, Bob came up to us. He then said something I never expected.

"I want you both to stay on in Farsund, full time. Don't answer me now. Bring your families out. Let them see too. My treat. Think about it. Talk it over. I'll visit the factory in a couple of weeks. I'll want an answer then."

"What about Kyle?" I asked. "Bob, you know he hates us. Don't you?"

The elephant in the room: Kentucky Kyle didn't like Bob, and he'd grown to dislike me too.

Bob had a dastardly smile on his face. "I just don't think you need to worry about that." True to Bob's words, we never did see Kentucky Kyle again.

Bob's offer was very generous, enough to seriously consider a life shift. Let my family visit Farsund, then they could see the beauty I was in love with; the place I'd lived all year.

CHAPTER 7

Bad Times

AUGUST 2008 TO JANUARY 2009

I had never seen anything like it. The whole world seemed to be in meltdown. Nothing felt real anymore. Everything I believed in, trusted, and relied upon was gone or going.

In the first week of October 2008, BMW cut all their orders by 40 percent overnight. Every other customer did the same. Then our bank went bankrupt a few days later. All our accounts were frozen. We had no order book, no money, and no way of paying our bills. This happened in just one week.

We heard talk of a "global financial crisis." The global financial system—the pillar of society, considered to be rock-solid and indestructible, way "too big to fail"—was dissolving like a snowball in a bucket of boiling water.

Wind the clock back two months.

I went to Annapolis to get my family. I needed them to see Farsund. I hoped it would be our new home. But my trip surprised Charlotte. I'd crashed her weekend plans. It was awkward. She hadn't expected me and already had a party to go to. I was added as her last-minute plus one.

"Who are these people?" I asked as she drove me down an unfamiliar road.

"You know the Baxters, darling, and the Hines. You've met them lots of times." The "darling" couldn't mask her frustration. But I had never met these people. They were Charlotte's friends, some of many I didn't know.

The party was already in full swing when we arrived at the lovely home nestled on the waterfront. All the windows and doors were open to the warm summer air. People spilled out onto the patio.

"Charlotte, darling!" shouted one woman. "Oh! And who's this handsome stranger?" The woman eyed me like a cut of meat.

"Now, Hillary," Charlotte replied in jovial chastisement. "This is my husband. Roger, meet Hillary. Hillary…"

The woman had already interrupted. "Come on, darling. They're all waiting for you." She grabbed Charlotte's hand and pulled her away into the kitchen. From the garden, I heard cheers and screams of joy over Charlotte's arrival. At that moment, standing alone, I realized she had another life, and she loved it. I had been away too long.

All of this became even more obvious once we got to Farsund. We talked and talked, weighing loads of different options. In the end, she finally said what I already knew she wanted.

"You love it here, darling." She gazed across the deep blue waters of the fjord surrounding the hotel. The view could not have been more spectacular, but she wasn't seeing it. She was focused intently on her message.

"Why don't you stay here? See if it works out. I'll look after the children and our home. You can come back anytime you want, darling."

She insisted we weren't separating, but it was obvious that bringing her to live in Norway would destroy her happiness and her new life. I didn't want to do that. So we agreed I'd settle into Farsund and visit home every six weeks. I would be a part-time Dad, but by making this sacrifice, I could support them all. Charlotte left the next day.

The summer evaporated. Farsund grabbed all my attention. My drive to grow the business shielded me from my faltering love life. To make matters worse, Tim decided not to stay. He wanted to be with his family.

I developed grand plans of building an empire in the midst of my loneliness. Pride, arrogance, and ignorance became my new companions. Like most fools, I didn't listen to anyone. I didn't pay attention to the markets. I blindly stuck to my own path. Sometimes, blindness can be good—until you run straight into a wall, full speed.

On September 15, 2008, the global financial crisis reared its very ugly head. The bankruptcy of Lehman Brothers catalyzed the near collapse of every financial system in the world. The ensuing Great Recession impacted every single industry, especially automotive, leaving devastation in its wake. GM was faltering, Saab was floundering, and Chrysler was in freefall.

How did it affect us? We were living off a credit card—an asset-based lending credit card. The bank, Landsbanki, would give us money every time we sold some parts. They set our credit limit against the value of our assets: our machines, our unsold parts, and any money our customers owed us. The bank would collect all the money that came in from our customers when they eventually paid us. They used the money to pay off our debt. The Money Men used our credit card to make the company run, called "working capital." It meant we had a big debt. Everything was okay if we kept selling enough to pay off our credit card. Then we could use it again.

At this point, we had about $2 million left on our card, which wasn't too bad a buffer for unexpected events. It's not just what you spend, though. It's what you earn. When you earn less than you did last month, your limit goes down. You run out of cash.

On October 4, it became clear we would earn less, much less. BMW slashed their orders by 40 percent, taking $4 million away from what we could earn—money we'd already spent.

We were going to run out of cash in a few months. My plans to grow the business suddenly looked pathetic.

Three days later, Landsbanki went bust. The Bank of England seized the assets but froze all our accounts. We had a little bit of money left in one Norwegian account, with just enough money to last us for one single week. We could still get to that.

The time to call Bob Baker again had arrived. I'd dealt with chaos throughout my career but nothing like I faced that bleak October day. Bob took my call early the next morning, remaining neutral as I delivered the critical news. I had one piece of good news to give: "I've spoken to Alan. He might have a way to turn the accounts back on. We'll know in a couple of days."

"That's a good thing," Bob said, his usual optimistic response.

"Yeah, it's okay, but we're up against our overdraft limits. There isn't really any cash available." I told him we'd already spent everything we had.

"Did you talk to Porsche? BMW? What did they say?" He'd asked me to beg both to pay early.

"Porsche doesn't owe us anything. BMW said they'll look into it. Actually, they're paying things late." BMW had blamed the crisis for delays in payment.

"Bob, there's one other thing. Someone fucked up. They sold the same invoice to the bank twice. It's about to roll off the account. Worse, it's a big one." We had invoiced BMW for some replacement tools—roughly a million bucks. Someone in my team accidentally entered it twice into our system, and we borrowed the full amount. Now we had to pay it back. We couldn't. We'd already run out.

"You've got to find new money, Roger." Bob could have screamed at me for spending too much; for being too naive; for letting this invoice screwup happen. But he didn't. He chose instead to state the obvious.

All I could do now was what I'd always done—mop up the mess. I'd start the day phoning all the government agencies. There had to be some money here. I went to the Ministry of Industry offices in Oslo, an agency in Trondheim, and another in Kristiansand and Stavanger.

When I wasn't begging for money, I was pleading for forgiveness. Every morning I'd meet with Knut Nesvold, my new financial manager, and Gordon Moskaland, my purchasing manager. We'd see if any money had come into our account. Then we'd look at the mounting backlog of bills we hadn't paid. We'd each take a list of vendors that wouldn't get paid and call them up with the bad news. We'd agree on our story in advance. It always sounded positive and hopeful. They just had to stay patient a little longer. The reaction was the same. Every vendor we called wanted to scream at us.

By the end of November, our usual meeting came to a head.

"This meeting has no purpose," Gordon stated, very calmly and clearly. "Every single supplier we have in Germany has cut us off. We can't make anything until we pay them. And we don't have any money, so we can't pay them."

I had gambled these suppliers wouldn't cut us off because doing so would cut BMW off. "How long until BMW finds out?" I asked in desperation. I had no idea what Frank Solbach and his team would do. Solbach chose which companies supplied BMW. He could make or break anyone he wanted to.

"They already know. Our suppliers have already told them." Gordon's usual steadiness masked the enormity of his message.

Solbach knew. Of course he did. I felt stupid thinking I could hide this from him. BMW functioned like a well-oiled management machine. They had radar everywhere, looking for any weaknesses in their supply chain. That explained why so many new faces had appeared, like Dr. Jurgen Schleinitz. I'd noticed he was suddenly copied on every email. I knew he was a lawyer, but I didn't know his role. On top of that, BMW had weekly meetings with the other German car manufacturers. They shared stories, consolidated risk, and planned for failure. They would do whatever was needed to protect their organizations and control their environment. If you hit their radar, it was likely they would run rather than help. Unfortunately, Farsund was blipping on their radar, bright and loud.

Meanwhile, the press wanted to report a story about sensational failure, something that would capture the havoc wreaked by the Great Recession. Farsund grabbed their attention. A company in the automotive industry and on the verge of collapse, owned by New York financial sharks—exactly what they were looking for. They had a ready-made protagonist too. I was fighting hard, knocking on the doors of every government agency, and begging for money. A grant, a loan, a fund… I didn't care. I just needed money.

The press loved it. The headlines of their first report announced, "Car Company in Crisis," a feature article on the factory. After that, it seemed every day there'd be another story about our instability and precarious financial position. Each time I flew to Oslo on a begging mission, the local newspaper or radio station would pick it up. Every little detail leaked, especially the bad stuff—exactly the sort of information BMW and Porsche were on the lookout for.

We limped on into December. I made what had become my daily call to Bob again. "Bob, this is bad. We are in real danger of going bankrupt. Our customers are going to have to react. I had a meeting with Porsche today. They're pissed with Alcoa too." Porsche felt they had been suckered into placing an order with Alcoa for a very unique part. They insisted Alcoa still had to make the part. They wouldn't let them transfer that order to the untrustworthy PE owners.

But Bob wasn't fazed. "So they know. I'm sure they've known for a long time. Good." I was perplexed.

He continued, clinically clear. "This is their problem. Porsche, BMW, even Alcoa. At least one of them is going to give us what we need. They don't build cars if we close our doors."

Bob's nonchalant response suddenly made me understand why the automotive industry didn't like private equity firms. It liked Mittelstand companies, those family-run German businesses who respected the authority and reputation of the customers. Bob and the rest of the Money Men in New York had adopted a casual attitude toward this whole event. They didn't care about the customer. Bob was sure BMW or Porsche would give us some money. If that didn't work, Alcoa would probably fund us or even buy us back. He was clear no money was coming from New York unless money came from someone else first.

"Go tell them, Roger. Go tell them to give you the money you need."

I'd worked out we needed about $4.5 million to get through this crunch. Bob wanted half to come from BMW and Porsche. He would get the rest from Congaree Capital but only once the others had committed to the deal. The money would keep us out of bankruptcy and allow me to start the factory again.

"Or Alcoa could buy back the company. They pay us $4 million, and they can have it."

This was Bob's world. He could turn mud into money.

All day, every day, I was trying everything I could think of. But our situation was only getting worse and worse. By mid-December I couldn't pay for anything. Our metal supply was cut off, so I couldn't make anything. It didn't actually matter at this point. Our machining suppliers in Germany had stopped sending our parts to the customers. Our component parts suppliers had stopped shipping parts to us. Even our local provider of cleaning services came and fetched their floor cleaning equipment. I laid off forty-five people and was on the verge of making everyone else redundant too. I only had enough money for the last payroll of the year.

When Christmas came, it didn't feel like the time to celebrate—not at the factory and not with my wife either. Our relationship was a wreck. I'd buried every problem. But I convinced myself at least I'd been successful at one thing: looking after my family. I didn't tell them anything. I kept the factory crisis hidden. They didn't have to worry about the consequences of my failure—not yet, anyway.

I flew back home on Christmas Eve. I was jet lagged and tired on Christmas morning, but nothing could dampen the magic of watching my kids rip open presents by the tree. Charlotte and I went out to walk our dogs in the woods in the afternoon. A cold mist hung in the air, and the overcast sky was frugal sharing light. Tension brewed between us as we made our way down the path, with the dogs sniffing, hunting, and searching in the leaves. It was time to talk.

I spoke first. "I sense something's changed between us. Do you feel it too?"

She looked relieved. I'd unleashed the subject. Now she could explain.

"You've been away so long. I can't just wait here, in limbo, putting my life on hold. I've made new friends, a new life. There isn't another lover. I'm not looking for that."

I knew it was true.

"My life goes on hold every time you come back." She was desperately revealing her feelings as openly as she could. "Who knows when this will finish?"

My heart sank. "I understand. It feels like I'm in your way. We love each other, but not in that way. We're really good friends now." I think saying that set her free.

Then she finalized it. "Love isn't important anymore. You're like a brother to me."

That's when my life changed. My marriage had crashed. I was devastated to lose my one true love. We were in a weird new world where I had to pretend she was a platonic friend. Of course she was a friend, but she was more than that. It felt like she was half of me. We had been "one" for more than twenty years. I tried to see the good in the situation. I needed anything that would make this okay. At least I could stay in contact with her, I reasoned. I couldn't let her down, and I didn't want to make her sad. I'd take anything I could get, even if it was a surreal friendship. It meant I'd still be in her life, and I could still be in my children's lives. I felt like I was still doing my job of looking after them too. It made me believe I had a purpose.

On Christmas night, I booked the last plane of the day and returned to Farsund. Somewhere over the Atlantic, around thirty-six thousand feet high, I slipped off my wedding ring. I never wore it again. But I kept it in my briefcase, just to remind myself it was never far away.

Christmas hadn't improved anything in Farsund. Every problem had patiently waited for me. The dark specter of bankruptcy loomed over the factory.

The Norwegian bankruptcy laws are quite clear and brutal. The law states a company can bankrupt if it is "insolvent and insufficient." In other words, you don't have the money to pay your bills or enough stuff you could sell to pay your bills. If you meet both of these conditions, the regional court declares you legally bankrupt, and you have to cease all operations. The business is then taken over by a government-appointed administrator, who winds up the business and closes it down for good. However, there is one potential recourse: If you've got a plan to acquire cash and pay what you owe, you can keep going. It just has to be a real, credible plan.

In the two weeks after Christmas, I worked hard to come up with exactly that type of plan. Finally, on Friday, January 9, 2009, I called Bob with positive news.

"Bob, both of them have agreed to our proposal. They'll match your money." I found it hard to believe my own words. Frank Solbach of BMW said he'd help us. If Porsche and BMW really gave us just over $2 million, then Bob had promised to match it. I would have enough money to pay my bills and get everything started again.

"Alcoa knows about this too," I continued. "I got a call this afternoon. Seems they are willing to give us metal again. The metal tap is back on, and we can restart production." This felt like my fairytale ending. Everyone would win.

"That's a good thing," Bob's signature comment was said with characteristic understatement. He had just gotten free money, once again proving his ability to squeeze blood from a stone. His carefree attitude testified to his power.

Private equity: one.

Automotive industry: zero.

But it was naive of me to imagine Bob had won. Solbach was simply buying time. There was no way he would let BMW hand over money to the New York sharks. He had other ideas.

I spent a week working with lawyers, accountants, and Bob to get everything ready. We all agreed Friday, January 16, 2009, would be the deadline to refinance the company. Bob told me New York was ready to wire money.

Then I got a call around 4:00 p.m. on that Friday. Solbach was on the other end. I'd been waiting all day for confirmation the money had been sent, but I didn't expect him to talk to me directly. BMW were difficult to deal with. They were big, complex, and powerful. They could make magic happen if they wanted, and Solbach was precisely the man who would do it.

"Mr. Cockroft, I want to talk to you with the strictest confidence. Can I assume you accept this condition?" It was as if he were reading from a well-worn script.

"Sure. We are in the cone of silence. Nothing gets out." I didn't know what he was about to divulge.

His English was nearly perfect, with only the slightest hint of a German accent. He sounded as if he were smiling, trying to keep a straight face and those gold-rimmed glasses on his pointy nose. "BMW will not invest in your company now. Your only option is to let the company go bankrupt."

This meant I'd have to fire everyone and hand the business over to a government administrator. We would be exposed to all sorts of risks I had no way of controlling. Solbach asserted BMW would protect the factory once the PE firm had been ousted. Then he'd find a new, benevolent owner to sweep us under their wings.

I felt as if I'd been punched in the gut.

"We will not support you any other way. We cannot work with your private equity partners."

His tone changed as he delivered his final words; his true feelings. "They are not right for this industry. We will give you long-term support if they are gone. Bankruptcy is the only way." He made it very clear he would not tolerate disobedience.

I was dazed as the call terminated. The company was undoubtedly qualified for bankruptcy. But I had spent this entire time trying to prevent that from happening. The only thing I could do now was to call Bob again.

Here I realized we stood on entirely different paths. Up until this point, we'd worked in unison. He'd been my mentor. Now, a different side to him emerged.

"Well, we just ride it to the end. Keep the business alive and put pressure on those bastards." I had never heard him swear before. Maybe Solbach was right. It seemed like Bob was too ruthless and too volatile. It felt like he refused to accept any situation he didn't control.

"I'm not going to break the law, Bob. We don't have a plan to get out of this. What about the people who work here? I don't have any money to pay them. I can't lie to them." I wasn't going to pretend they'd still get paid. I couldn't decide if Bob had actually considered the implications of what he'd just said. His next words eliminated my residual doubt.

"I don't care about that. I guess the government will look after them. This happens all the time. You'll be okay too. I'm sure you'll find a way back home."

It suddenly dawned on me Bob was prepared to crash this company hard unless he got free money. It seemed he was more worried about his reputation within Wall Street than Farsund. Nothing could have angered me more, but I didn't want to react. I had to think; to bide my time; to plan.

Bob chimed in, breaking the awkward silence. "Let me work on this over the weekend. I'll come back with a plan Monday morning," I agreed.

I was going to have to wrestle the company out of his control. As much as I hated to admit it, bankruptcy was my only choice. I would follow Solbach's plan. I didn't know if I could trust him, but I knew I couldn't trust Bob and the New York PE guys. Bankruptcy would allow me to pick up the pieces and rebuild something. I had to keep my team, and I needed the backing from Porsche and BMW. Solbach would have to be the key. I had nothing without his support. By the end of the weekend, I had a plan and was ready to go.

Monday came, and as I expected, Bob had nothing to offer. We had reached a stalemate. I pulled in lawyers and accountants to back up my claim we were bankrupt, but Bob refused to listen. So on Tuesday, I called Frank Solbach.

"I'm about to bankrupt this business, as you urged me to do. I need to know you'll support me, and BMW will keep their orders with Farsund and help me save the factory." I wanted to be absolutely precise. Solbach may have hated the private equity guys, but did he care at all about Farsund?

"You have my word, Mr. Cockroft. I want you to be our agent. Tell me everything that is going on. We'll search for a suitable new owner." He sounded clinical and a little hasty. Did I trust him? I only had one choice: Solbach and my customers, or Bob and the New York sharks. The choice was ugly, but Solbach was the best I had.

Next, I made another call to Bob. "Nothing changed, I assume?" Bob confirmed New York had no intention of putting in any money. So I continued with my plan.

"Then I will recommend we file for bankruptcy this week. If you don't agree, l have no option but to resign in protest."

I don't think Bob thought I was going to be that aggressive, because his only response was, "You've got to decide whose side you're on." I was definitely burning my New York bridges.

But I'd already made my decision and had one last trick to play. I wanted to get money to pay the January paychecks. "Didn't the insurance pay you out for that metal spill thing? That was last week. Wasn't it?" Bob knew where I was going. "Send that money to me, and I can make payroll. Then I'll support your plan." Would he bite?

He did. He wired $400,000 across that day. As soon as it landed, I cut paychecks for everyone, actually earlier than normal, and got the money into the hands of the team.

The time to prepare the Norwegian system to expect bankruptcy had come. The court room looked modern and ominous. A row of desks lined the walls of the octagonal room. The judge's seat and desk were raised higher than the others, anchoring the center. The royal crest adorned the wall behind his chair, which was empty. Knut and I were waiting for the judge to join us. It would be an informal meeting, but it felt like we were about to be tried under oath. Eventually the judge walked in.

Once we introduced ourselves, I got underway. "You need to know the details. It will help you make decisions later." I laid down printed copies of our financials and cash forecasts. We delved into the technicalities.

"Why are you telling me this?" he asked suspiciously.

"Bankruptcy is the only chance of saving the factory. We're running out of time before we lose customer support." I paused as I thought. "And we need the best administrator we can get."

Knut chimed in, "This is the guy we want. Håvard Wiker." He showed the judge a printout of Wiker's profile. "I hear he's good—very good. Can you see if he's available?"

The judge listened but didn't agree. "I need a complaint from one of your creditors to start the bankruptcy process. It's hard to find someone in Farsund to do that. A complaint is public, and blame for sinking our factory will follow." He was right, of course. Farsund remembers people's actions.

My next step: I left the court house and drove to meet the general manager of the metal factory. I knew he couldn't file the complaint I needed without getting corporate approval, so I asked him to bring along the owner of another company that we owed money. This person could complain to the court. He could make decisions himself. My job was to convince them it was the right thing to do.

"We are bankrupt. You know that. We won't survive under the New York guys. I can't file. I don't have the board's approval. I need one of you to complain to the court. We owe you money, and I can't pay you."

Roy, the general manager of the metal factory, asked in curiosity, "What are you going to do? How can you make this any better?"

"I have the support from BMW and Porsche. If I get rid of New York, we can relaunch or get someone to buy the factory. If we don't go bankrupt, Bob and his team will destroy any hope of a future." It was a solemn message.

I turned to the owner of the other company, Arne Marthensen. "It has to be you, Arne. I need your help. Please."

"Let us think about this." It was clear they both wanted to talk without me.

Back to New York: I sent an email spelling out again we were bankrupt, with my letter of resignation attached. Then I waited.

Bob's phone call came less than a minute after I'd hit send. For the first time, his calm exterior had shattered. He started to yell at me. Even worse, I'd tricked him into handing over all that money on the promise I *would* accept his path.

I had one weakness, though. It would take several days for the bankruptcy cogs to start spinning. Bob would have control until then, and he might do something crazy if he found out. He could make his complaint go away. He might put just enough money into the company to keep it like a zombie, not quite dead but definitely not alive. Then he could use it to terrorize my two main customers. The whole bankruptcy thing had to hit Bob by surprise and off guard. Once the courts declared bankruptcy, Bob was out. I had to distract him.

"I'd like you to keep my medical insurance for six months, please. Can you pay for my rental for six months too?" I continued. "How are you going to pay for my relocation back to the US?"

He bit. "You don't get anything. I want you gone at the end of the week." That was the two days I needed. I would use those days well.

The following day, I issued a statement to the employees. I knew this would be the fastest way to attract the press.

Thursday, January 22, 2009

On Wednesday afternoon I had no choice but to resign from Casting Technologies Farsund. I took this step because I feel the company is insolvent and the chairman does not support my recommendation to file for bankruptcy. I have no intention of trading while insolvent.

This decision wasn't easy but essential to preserve the facility and the jobs for our community. We must preserve our integrity and customers' respect. Prolonging a decision helps no one.

Within minutes I had an army of press at the door. That evening the story made it on the national TV channel. And the next morning all the papers carried it, with headlines proclaiming I had quit in protest.

I left the office on Friday evening. It was my last day working for Bob. I was almost late for an off-the-record meeting with the editor of the *Farsund Avis*. As we sat in his office, the snow fell in thick flakes outside. Winter had returned to Farsund. The room was small and ill-lit, but it was warm as we huddled around his table.

I spelled out the options for the paper. No one knew yet bankruptcy loomed for the factory. I didn't want anyone to be blamed for that, especially not Arne who had been brave enough to file the complaint.

"You can tell the bankruptcy story now. Breaking news! The complaint has been filed, and it's public information. You can find out who filed the complaint at the court too." I looked him dead in the eye. "I don't want you to do that. It will hurt my only chance of saving this thing. If the New York guys find out, they could screw this up."

It would be too late for them to do anything by the time the court told them they were bankrupt. They would either have to inject millions of bucks to reverse that decision or just walk away. I was guessing they'd do the latter.

"The option I'd like you to consider is you work with me. You can wait until the court declares bankruptcy. That will be one story. Then the administrator will be appointed. Then the company restarts production. And finally it gets relaunched. I can promise you will have all four of these stories first. I can make sure you get every story before anyone else, but only if you work with me."

I was winging it, but I needed them. And I could sense he wanted to cooperate.

I left the editor to ponder my proposal. What next? I had to pack. I had to go off the radar. I couldn't have any contact with Bob or his colleagues; nowhere near the press, the lawyers, or anyone. That way I couldn't be quoted, cited, or sued. The bankruptcy process would proceed without my involvement. Then I thought, *Where should I go?*

The snow had collected quickly on the streets. It compacted under my boots as I walked to my apartment. The crunching sound reminded me of skiing with my family in Chamonix, my favorite resort. I was out of a job again and taking big risks that could go awry at any moment. Chamonix would give me the calm I needed before the storm.

CHAPTER 8

Any Road, Every Road

JANUARY TO APRIL 20, 2009

The Pointe Isabelle Hotel is nestled in the heart of Chamonix. It isn't grand by any stretch of the imagination, but it has a comfortable family feel and affords spectacular views of the mountains. My phone buzzed as I savored the twilight scenery out on the tiny hotel balcony. Knut had sent me a text, the first time he'd contacted me that week.

Can you call me please? This was the message I'd been waiting for.

"Evening, Knut. Tell me what's happening." I didn't even know if the company had gone into bankruptcy.

"Have I got a story to tell you!" Knut was excited, engaged, and high-spirited—already a good sign.

"Well, first tell me: Did we file? Did we go bankrupt?"

"Oh, yeah, yeah, yeah, we did that. That was Tuesday. It was in all the papers." The *Farsund Avis* had gotten its first story, as I'd promised. But today was Thursday, and the bankruptcy was already history for Knut. He had much more to tell me.

"Did we get Wiker? Is he our administrator? What's he like?" I was holding Knut from his news, bombarding him with questions, but I needed to know all the details.

"Oh, yes," he said in a matter of fact. "We got him and his team. Mr. Wiker is a very assured person. He knows exactly what he's doing and does not compromise."

So the press had its second story, too, but the way Knut said it made me wonder. *Perhaps Wiker's too hard?*

Knut wouldn't give me time to ponder. Finally unleashed, he dove into his update. "Let me tell you what happened today. We had a full house. BMW had three, and there were two from Porsche. Even someone from Ferrari was there. They all came to see Wiker. I sat them in the customer room. Wiker made them wait all day.

"I felt like I had to wait with them," Knut said. "It was probably the most awkward meeting. We couldn't even offer them lunch. We're bankrupt."

"So you starved them?" I was seeing why Knut had giggled.

"It was Roth who finally snapped. He grumped this had gone on far too long. He demanded to see Wiker." Knut sounded mischievous as he revealed the punch.

He continued, "Exactly at that moment, Wiker walks in. He's a tall guy. He looks strong, determined. He has a way of drawing your attention simply from the look on his face. Not someone to be messed with. It shut Roth down.

"I put on my grandest tone and said, 'Well, here he is now. Ladies and gentlemen, this is Mr. Håvard Wiker, the government-appointed administrator.' Wiker didn't even say hi! Nothing! He just stood at the door and said, 'I'm not here to negotiate.'" He mimicked Wiker's authoritative voice.

"Solbach didn't listen. He started his own dialogue. He wanted to take center stage. He was BMW, the big boy at the table. He said, 'Ahhh, Mr. Wiker. We received your proposal. I must say it seems extravagant. I'd like to discuss…' but Wiker cut him off." Knut portrayed Solbach in a Gollum-style voice. It sounded right.

"Wiker just repeated what he'd said. He told them the company would close if they didn't put $2.6 million into his account no later than first thing in the morning as a security. He was very precise and spelled out *two point six million dollars*. Then he told them he was late for his plane and left."

Wiker was definitely the right guy. "I wished I could have seen that. Sounds bloody hilarious. Then what happened?"

"You won't believe this. They all scrambled to their phones. They actually made wires within less than thirty minutes."

Suddenly Knut's jollity ended. "Since then it's been a nightmare. Wiker's making me control everything. Solbach told him they want you to help them sell the business. So Wiker wants to see you Tuesday morning." His tone conveyed some hope.

As I listened, I gazed out over Chamonix city center. Night had crept in. The lights made the frosted buildings shimmer. The New York Money Men were out. Wiker was in charge now. He represented the Norwegian government—transparency. Wiker was tough to deal with, though. He wouldn't budge. Both Frank Solbach and Martin Roth needed someone they could control—an insider. I was their man. That gave me a door back into the game. It was exactly what I had planned for.

For my Tuesday meeting with Wiker, we'd agreed to meet for coffee in the Rederiet Hotell. To show respect, I'd dressed in a suit and tie. We were both about the same height and build. The sofa we chose felt a little snug, so Wiker moved to another chair as we settled in. I didn't know what to expect, but I hid my fears and focused on him.

He leaned into the table and took a sip of coffee. With a wry smile on his face he said, "In my line of work, I rarely see the CEO after bankruptcy. Yet here you are. I've rarely been told by the customers that the CEO would be their liaison. Yet they did. I've never been asked to reappoint the old CEO by all the employees. Yet they are begging me to reinstate you."

He paused. "Who are you, Mr. Cockroft? Why are you here?"

This marked the start of one of the most successful partnerships I've ever experienced. Wiker exceeded all my expectations. He wasn't just a good lawyer. He was the definitive bankruptcy lawyer in Norway. He single-handedly wrote most of the laws and multiple books on the subject.

He had three priorities to consider: the creditors—people the company owed money to—the employees, and the community the company supported. He had six months of absolute control over every asset the company had. The company could stay alive as long as he had enough cash and a reason to keep it operating. It was time to fix this.

I was surprised by how good it felt to walk into the factory the next morning. My office felt like home. Helge wasted no time in poking his head around my door.

"Welcome back! It's good to have you in charge again."

"I'm not in charge. Wiker and Knut are leading this." I didn't want to step on any of Wiker's orders. I didn't want to upset him in any way. "I'm just here to try and help sell what remains of the factory."

"Well, maybe not the CEO," Helge said as he digested my response, "but at least he's not here anymore." He pointed to a pair of work boots tucked under a chair. I hadn't noticed them until now. They were Stanley Cuttle's. He'd been sent by the Money Men to manage things while Bob tried to wrestle the company back under their control. Stanley retreated quickly when Bob lost. His abandoned boots were a symbol of just how close my plan was to failure. They also symbolized that I could win if I just didn't stop trying. Good things would happen to good people eventually. I would keep Stan's shoes there for the next three years as a reminder.

"Helge, how many people came back? How many are working at the factory?" I was confined to my office only. I couldn't go into the factory and see for myself. It would be overstepping my boundary.

"Oh, about sixty people, or there abouts." He rocked his head side to side as he pondered the number.

"What? That's crazy. Why so few? Where is the technical team? What's going on?" Most of the team had been sacked. I'd lose the company's brain if I lost key staff.

Helge knew what I was thinking. "I heard from the NAV that National Oilwell is bringing a recruiting team into town next week." He looked very concerned.

NAV, the Norwegian Labour and Welfare Administration, had a duty. They looked after people and made sure they got benefits if they didn't have a job. They were solid benefits, too, with 60 percent of what they used to earn—a reliable social safety net. But benefits would stop if you didn't take a job you could do.

Norway had a very strong need for technical experts: scientists, engineers, mechanical technicians. The oil industry would swallow them up in a heartbeat. The National Oilwell company had jobs available for every single one of them.

Helge moved into my office and slumped into a seat. "Oil jobs are hard. Three or four weeks offshore! I wouldn't do it." He shook his head and then turned to me. "They've got a hard choice to make if they don't have a job here. But they'll be under pressure: Take a new job or lose all their benefits."

I knew we could be dead in days. So I asked for help from Almar Friestad, the local industry liaison officer. Almar was a true Norwegian troll of a man, huge but gentle. He didn't have any pretense about his position. But that Wednesday evening, my first back at the factory, he occupied a pivotal role. I spent that evening working with him, talking him through my dilemma.

"I'm having no luck finding the right people. The NAV is a nightmare to navigate," I explained in frustration.

Almar made a phone call. He had the power to summon the right people. People I'd been trying to contact all day suddenly appeared as if by magic. They shared the same office block. It's always who you know.

In Norwegian, Almar explained the situation clearly. Then he switched to English. "We can sell the cream, but at what cost? The milk will surely spoil." What he meant was the issue wouldn't be the engineers or technical staff. "What about those less qualified? How will they find jobs if this factory closes?"

He got NAV to give me two weeks, during which they would turn a blind eye to all the workers my technical team took. They would continue to pay out benefits to all those who had alternate job offers. Two weeks to get them all back on the payroll of a bankrupt company, with no clear future. NAV bent the rules generously, and that gave me time to solve this new problem.

Wiker and his partner, Erik Sandtrø, met me the next morning. Erik seemed to be a younger, thinner, and shorter model of Wiker, with every bit of his cleverness.

"Last night NAV gave me two weeks. I need your help. I've got an idea." My plan would totally change what Wiker had already established.

"What if I come up with a budget for the people I'll need to run this business? I'll break it down by customer. Porsche can pay for the development team. They'll be working only for Porsche…" I had a deceptive smirk on my face, "…ish."

"I'm listening," Wiker said. He didn't like being forced to entertain a request until he felt ready. Once he'd prepared himself and opened his mind, you'd get his undivided attention. But if you tried to push it, he'd shut you down. So it was a good thing he was listening to me now.

"We can ask each customer to guarantee up to six months of all costs specifically associated with their business. If they buy into that scheme, they get their parts at their normal price. If they don't, we charge them double for any part they need."

Erik started to play with the idea. "I like this. We will have to have break clauses, of course." If things went wrong, Wiker still had to be able to cut all agreements.

"Will you manage this, Mr. Cockroft? I don't have time or interest." Wiker was asking me to take back control of the company. He trusted me. He was supporting me.

On February 14, 2009, BMW, Porsche, and Ferrari signed a new six-month contract, their Valentine's Day present to Farsund. My plan worked. They had to put another $3 million in an escrow account to secure production. Then they could have a supply of parts at their normal sales price. Other customers, like Volvo, were forced to pay twice the normal price for their parts. Wiker immediately reinstated me as CEO. All three customers endorsed his decision, and I instantly rehired my full team.

The next morning the local newspaper headlined the news, featuring a very cheesy picture of me standing outside the factory in the snow in the middle of the night. I looked like Wallace from the cartoon *Wallace and Gromit*. I had both thumbs held high, and the paper's headlines quoted me declaring everything was going to be okay.

My message was clear: We could get out of this. Indeed, the following week we started production again, and the *Farsund Avis* had its third story, as promised. One more story to go.

"Du," Hilde Rullestad said. In Norwegian, the word "du" means "you," and it's used to get your attention. Hilde managed the company's logistics. She made sure every customer got exactly what they ordered. I was making a late-night grocery run, pushing my shopping cart along the aisles.

"Don't fuck this up." She certainly got my attention. She wasn't cross, just more desperate.

"Evening, Hilde, and thank you for your kind words," I quipped. She was a super bright person who I admired, a single mother with a fighting spirit. She was also beautiful in a true Scandinavian sense.

"If you fail we lose hard. It might be inconvenient for you. Maybe you miss a vacation or something—trivial stuff until you find your next job."

She paused and let me catch up with her. "It's not like that for most of us. There aren't any jobs in Farsund. Without this wage, we'd have to make hard decisions, like how to feed our families and what meal we cut out each day, or worse: move away from here." I looked at her cart. It was virtually empty. Only the bare essentials.

"We depend on you winning. I don't know why you're fighting, but don't stop. Try harder."

I hadn't truly grasped how much this meant to the people of Farsund. Her words galvanized me. I made a vow right then. *I will not fail. Farsund will win. I will not let them down.* This was personal.

On April 20, I sat in a meeting room in Trondheim, trying to calm down. Ten minutes until I presented my plan to relaunch the factory under new owners; ten minutes until a decision would finally be made; ten minutes until I'd find out the fate of my promise to Hilde and the rest of Farsund.

Wiker stood by my side. In fact, he'd been by my side all through spring. He began asking me a series of questions to test my preparation. "Did Roth or Solbach get back to you? Did they tell you why none of their candidates show any interest in buying the factory?"

"Nothing new, no. I guess it's just the wrong time to sell. Everyone is out of cash. This recession is a long way from being over. People are scared, and scared people don't take risks."

I'd hosted a slew of candidates that BMW and Porsche had encouraged to visit the factory. I did everything Solbach told me to do. Some visitors came as a favor to Solbach or Roth. Others just came to get the inside scoop on our process. None had any intention of buying the factory.

Failure frustrated Solbach at first. He set deadlines in February and March, threatening to cut all orders if no one bought the business. The threat was a direct challenge to Porsche and Roth, as well as Farsund. Roth had no alternatives. Porsche needed Farsund to make their new part. The threat motivated me to find an alternative.

That's when I came up with my own idea. I could do what my dad did. I could buy the company. Solbach seemed to support it, which felt encouraging because I needed all the customers to back my plan, especially BMW, our largest source of revenue. But Ferrari and Porsche had to stay too. All told, they represented about $54 million a year. We needed every dollar.

I'd spent months selling this idea. BMW had scrutinized every aspect, insisting I make a slew of changes. I'd agreed and accommodated every single request. Now was the last hurdle: the big investors. This was the final meeting with the CEO of Investinor, a government fund. If Investinor agreed, other regional funds would follow.

The team walked in, and my make-it-or-break-it moment arrived. I recognized Jan Hassel, my sponsor, straight away. I'd spent months convincing him of my plan. Then I spied the CEO, the head of this $600 million investment fund.

I glanced at Wiker, took a deep breath, and tried to look as calm as I could. "Gentlemen, I won't keep you longer than needed today. The crux of my vision is people—specifically, Farsund folk. For many years, Farsund has depended on innovative industries based in the heart of the town.

"Those industries truly push the boundaries of what was considered possible. Credibility in the automotive world is one flag they can raise. The car parts factory leads the technical world there." They were listening.

"The company and its employees have hit a hard rock, though, bankruptcy through a combination of ill fate and careless ownership.

"We can fix this. I have a plan I'd like to present today." I looked at Wiker, and he nodded his approval. Everyone at the table knew him and his reputation. His endorsement boosted my persuasive power.

I proceeded to lay out my plan in all its detail. I'd relaunch the factory, keep my big automotive clients, and expand by selling new products into different industries. They all had questions, mostly about my commitment and credibility. I explained I was investing my own money, and this would be my sole focus. I would be there full time.

Things had gone well, but I didn't want to sound overly optimistic as I reached the last part of my speech. "The plan, my proposal, will work. I believe in it. I'm investing my money. Håvard believes in it." Again, he nodded.

"The staff all believe in it, and so does the wider community. They're all investing." This was my last piece.

"BMW, Porsche, and Ferrari believe in it too. They will keep their business with us. They all support us. Håvard can confirm this." Every face turned to Wiker. Again he gave his confirmation.

"The last question I have: Will you back my plan? Will you back Farsund?"

Silence. Then Jan asked for a moment with his team. Wiker and I were left alone. Seconds turned to minutes. Minutes seemed like hours. We sat in silence.

Finally Jan led the team back into the room. He cleared his throat then began, "You understand your industry is not a focus for our investment fund. Further, we have not made a single investment since the fund was launched in January. These two things make it very difficult for us." My heart was in free fall.

"But your plan is compelling. Mr. Wiker's support is impressive. Your reputation is sound, and your objective is honorable." I held on to his every word.

"Provided you can show us proof of your customers' commitments over the next five years, then we support you. Congratulations on being the first to receive approval for investment from Investinor."

Champagne corks, fireworks, roars of joy—at least, that's what I imagined in my head. Farsund had a future. We just had one last formality to complete: support from BMW, Porsche, and Ferrari for five years. *That should be easy,* I thought. They'd all been part of this plan. Wiker offered to pen the letters and have them signed by the end of month, on April 30, 2009.

CHAPTER 9

Bug Squashing

——

APRIL 30, 2009

"They always kill the little ones first," Karsten Mohr said as he drove me from the airport to the BMW offices. His eyes, framed by oval gold-rimmed glasses, were fixed on the busy road ahead.

"What the hell are you talking about?"

"That's what they do. If things get bad, they save the big ones and kill the little ones," he said. He always had a smile that made his eyes squint, as though he were about to crack a joke. I wish he was.

"I'm hearing some rumors from our tooling guys. It sounds like there's another three sets of tools being made for the new five and seven series parts, and they're bound for Italy."

My mind was racing. "Are you sure this is for the same parts?" It would be crazy to be doing this, right now, when there was a way out of this problem. New tools cost millions of dollars. This had to be wrong.

Tools are complex, highly specialized casting molds whereby molten aluminum is turned into a cast part. They are unique to every cast part and will last for hundreds of thousands of cycles. We had a maintenance team in house that could fix the tools but not make them. Only a few special companies could make tools. They didn't make parts, just the tools. There aren't too many of them either. We all use them, so it's a good place to pick up industry gossip.

As he drove into Munich, Karsten continued, "The engineers over at the tool makers called me this morning, boss. They said Mazzucconi [an Italian competitor] had inquired how long it would take to make a set of three dies. They didn't get a drawing, but it sounded like they were for the seven series."

"They didn't place an order then?" I asked. Before Karsten could answer I continued, "BMW are just looking for options in case my plan doesn't work."

Of course that's what was happening, I reasoned. If I were in BMW's shoes, I'd want to know my alternatives. After all, we were in bankruptcy. I tried to ignore the fact today was the deadline Wiker had set for all parties to commit to Farsund. Porsche and Ferrari had already complied, but Solbach had summoned me to meet him in Munich at 5:00 p.m. I was still optimistic about our collaboration as we drove up to the FIZ, BMW's Research and Innovation Center.

The FIZ had been designed in the early '80s when BMW sat at the cutting edge of technology. Their glory was reflected in the design of the building. Trees skirted the concrete courtyard just off the main road. Each tree poked up through square holes cut into the concrete. A fleet of flags flew in front of the building, and a sweeping set of steps led toward the entrance. As I looked up, I marveled at the glass atrium that transitioned into glass-fronted offices. The ceilings soared fifty feet high while a cutaway floor revealed two more subterranean levels.

But tight budgets and dwindling profits hadn't been easy. Much of the interior still dated back to the '80s and bore more than twenty years of wear. The offices were tired.

The employees matched the offices, too, dressed as if stuck in the past: brown Hush Puppies, synthetic fiber slacks, dull avocado-colored button-down shirts, and bland brown and green ties.

It felt like they had a culture of principles. *Survive, don't thrive. Keep your head down, and make sure you don't make any mistakes. It's better to do nothing than make a mistake. Above all, respect the hierarchy, which is closely guarded and controlled.* At the top of this middle management sat Frank Solbach. This was his kingdom. Away from the super elite leadership, he lorded over the "forgotten lands."

One of Solbach's minions met Karsten and me at the reception after we'd surrendered our identification documents. Once we'd negotiated the security gates, he gave us a meeting room number and then disappeared. Any sense of grandeur vanished once we passed through security. We now faced a labyrinth of corridors, each one looking exactly like the next. Every level had identical tan-colored walls, doors, and linoleum flooring. Without a guide, it would have been easy to get lost for hours.

Karsten reassured me, "Don't worry, boss. I know the layout. I've been here a thousand times." So off we went. Karsten sported his familiar optimistic smile as he led the way. I'd been here a number of times, too, but I was lost instantly. Soon enough, Karsten seemed to be lost too.

We now had fewer than five minutes to find the room. After establishing it wasn't on the top floor, we went down to the next level. But nothing there matched the room code we'd been given either. After consulting one of the fading maps at the corridor intersection, we deduced our meeting room was in the basement. We pushed through a set of dark brown, double doors into a hidden corridor. We were immediately hit by the smell of warm dust.

By now I was sure we were lost. But then Karsten said, "Here we go, boss. This is our room." It looked like a boiler room. As we entered, we were greeted by Hans Saller. He'd been the first person I'd met at BMW back in 2008. Now, at the end of his career, Saller seemed like he was ready to quit the BMW bullshit.

Karsten and I did our best to ignore our surroundings and just sat quietly, waiting.

Time ticked slowly by. Then Hans suddenly broke the silence with his deep voice. "Bavarian bulls. BMW uses Bavarian bull leather to cover their steering wheels. Do you know why?" We didn't. "In Bavaria we don't use barbed wire. There are no marks or gouges in the leather hide. We use bulls because cows get pregnant, and they get stretch marks. Bulls don't get stretch marks. We make steering wheels in Bavaria and ship them all over the world, including South Africa. That's how deeply we care about quality at BMW." I really wasn't sure what to say.

Five minutes later the BMW team arrived, led by Solbach. Behind him was his sidekick, Reinhold Hierl, and someone I'd never met before but whose name I knew well: Dr. Jurgen Schleinitz, a member of the legal team for BMW. Short but distinguished, he was clearly a corporate guy, much farther up the tree. *Why was he here?* I thought. Maybe because I'd asked them to sign a binding commitment. I was trying to be optimistic.

They all seated themselves on one side of the meeting table, farthest away from the door. Solbach picked up a copy of my presentation and donned his small reading glasses. He then pushed back from the table as if to disengage himself from the meeting before it had even started. Undeterred, I plowed into my presentation.

"Thank you for finding time to meet with us today." I made sure to maintain eye contact with Solbach.

"I know this isn't new news, but it's great we finally have a plan and the cash to relaunch the company. I'll go over it again today at a high level. We've just got enough revenue to make this work. New capital is coming too. We're all investing in the factory along with the Norwegian government agencies." Their faces remained expressionless. This should have been good news for them: government-supported, stable supplier, out of bankruptcy. My heart began to pound.

"You've already agreed to stay with us for the next five years. The one request the agencies have asked is each major customer sign this letter, solidifying your agreement." I held a copy of the letter that Wiker had sent them the previous week.

"If we keep all our orders, we can do this. But every single order counts. Five years gives us time to win new business, new customers, maybe new markets too. We become more stable and a better supplier."

I wanted to strike the right balance between sounding loyal and proving we were innovative, growing, and learning. "BMW will always be number one to us, but we will diversify our customer base, become less dependent on you. That will reduce both of our risk of something like this bankruptcy happening ever again."

By this point, I was just repeating myself. The BMW team in front of me had already been through every step of this plan. They knew exactly what I needed. They had agreed verbally. Now I was just asking for something in writing.

"Mr. Wiker sent you that letter last week. He asked for your written commitment by April 30. Today. I've already got the same commitment from the Porsche team and from

Ferrari. So let me dive into the presentation pack. You can sign this letter at the end." Solbach glanced at Hierl and then Schleinitz. He had a furtive smile, holding the presentation pack in front of his face like a shield.

I tried to ignore these warning signs and just kept pushing forward. I detailed how we could expand business outside of the automotive industry. I detailed my business plan and pointed out the advantages of having Norwegian government oversight through Investinor being on board.

I finished my speech—silence; not one question. Then Hierl leaned forward with his hands clasped together and resting on the table in front of him. His lips puckered as he prepared to speak.

In broken English, he stated matter-of-factly, "Mr. Cockroft, after much consideration we have determined we are going to change our business relationship with you." He sounded as if he'd practiced his speech earlier in the day.

"We will keep the contract for the current model five and seven series with you until the end of build." That was the end of this year. Everything was okay so far; what I expected. I examined Hierl's face for any clue, but I couldn't detect much. He was simply reading his script, focused on making sure he didn't miss a word.

"We will keep the contract for the current model Mini, and you will supply 70 percent of the parts we need." Still good news. Nothing had changed.

Tension filled the room. Behind his reading glasses, Solbach's eyes widened. *Here it comes.*

"We won't return the contract for the current one series to you." This was a blow. We'd been making these parts for years. My mind raced to think of a way to fill the revenue gap this created.

"We won't return the contract for the current three series to you." This was a bigger volume. I started to feel stunned.

"We won't return the contract for the new model seven series to you." The new model seven was the second biggest contract. I sat silently and showed no emotion. *I'll keep my dignity, thank you.* I held on tightly, punch after punch after punch.

"We have decided we won't return the contract for the new model five series to you." Our biggest contract, gone. It didn't matter now. We'd already lost too much business unless there was good news. *Would they give us some new orders?*

In the deafening silence, Hierl checked his script one more time. A look of satisfaction spread across his face. He'd completed his task. No more news, good or bad.

Solbach, however, had to make one final comment, one last dig. Picking up a point I'd made earlier in my presentation, he stated sarcastically, "We will help you become less dependent on BMW as a customer." For the first time he leaned forward as he said this, still keeping his spindly legs crossed. His tone sounded patronizing, like that of a father teaching his young child too much candy was bad. Then they all smiled.

"Shock" doesn't fully describe the stew of emotions I felt right then. BMW had decided to take away 70 percent of our business—exactly what I relied on to restart the company. Now my plan lay in ruins. The fact they never had any intention of supporting us was obvious now. They had simply needed three months to find alternate suppliers. They had pretended to support our plan, keeping us busy and out of their way while finding someone else to replace us.

As professionally as I could, I gathered up my things, folded away my laptop, and picked up the presentation packs they'd discarded. The optimism had drained from Karsten's face. For once he carried a look of resignation. We exited the dungeon-like room.

As Karsten led us through the maze of corridors back toward the atrium, he tried to talk to me. "What do we do now, boss? Who do we…" His voice sounded like I'd never heard before, warbling in a higher register.

I cut him off. "Say nothing, look relaxed, and let's get out of here."

They'd played me every step of the way. I'd let them bring most of our competitors to come and see our process to essentially steal our secrets. I'd kidded myself these might be people who would buy our factory. In reality, they were just here to copy what we did and then let us die.

I was mad at myself for letting this happen. I'd been too focused on getting the business plan together. I'd assumed

BMW was telling the truth, and now I looked like an ass. We said nothing as we walked back along the corridors to the reception and checked ourselves out of the FIZ.

Karsten and I turned toward the parking garage and paused in front of the glass atrium. "Give me a cigarette," I said. We stopped and lit up. I didn't smoke, but I needed the nicotine to calm my mind. It was turning like a tornado.

The cigarette did its trick. Now my mind was focused. I felt angry, alive, and full of energy. I looked at Karsten and exhaled.

"Those bastards. I'm going to make them pay millions for this." I sounded resolute, but I actually didn't have a clue what I was going to do. All I knew was I had to win.

CHAPTER 10

The Lightbulb

MAY 5, 2009

I heard the sound of stilettos clicking on the sidewalk as Karin Degler confidently strode into the guard house to pick me and Wiker up. Impeccably dressed in dark business attire, Degler always looked on point.

She walked us out of the factory and back onto the street, Porsche Platz, and then down the hill to a meeting room in another building. It could have seated thirty people, but today there were just five: me, Håvard Wiker, Martin Roth, Karin Degler, and Stephen Spreiter, the purchasing guy responsible for choosing Farsund when it belonged to Alcoa. Wiker and I were there to report BMW's decision to effectively close us down.

We all took our seats around the U. The Porsche team stared back at me intently, waiting for my explanation of how I would fix this. They all appeared the same—professional, stylish, intelligent, and very sharp—except for one small crack. Roth was hunched over a note pad scribbling, with his lower jaw clenched and protruding. He didn't like uncertainty. Though he contained his anger well, I could detect it clearly in that moment.

"Look, I need some time to think about what I can do," I said. "The urgent threat is we will lose our key players. As soon as this gets out, we're over.

"We'll certainly lose our engineers straight away," I added. "Let me think, and we can talk later in the week. Martin, this is important. Please see if you can use anyone in your network to persuade Solbach to change his decision."

We broke up after less than thirty minutes. The office was at the bottom of the Platz, not far from the famous Porsche Museum. Porsche's bitter rival, Daimler, had a museum in Stuttgart too. Like territorial flags, these museums claimed authority in the city. CEO Wendelin Wiedeking had built the Porsche Museum on the north side of Stuttgart, and it opened in January of 2009. He made sure his was bigger and more impressive, honoring the Porsche family history. The artistically engineered building was elevated on pillars, with beautiful glass frontage and asymmetrical walls. It was both formidable and breathtaking.

We had time to kill before our flights, so Wiker decided to go take a look at the museum. "Besides, there's a very well-known steak house on the top floor," he said, "and I'm hungry."

The museum experience was designed around an upward spiral representing time, with over three hundred cars on display. The base represented the founding history, including the Porsche tractors and Ferdinand Porsche's original design of the VW Beetle. As I ascended the spiraling ramp, I saw breakout areas on each floor showcasing the launch of Porsche, the evolution of the iconic 911, Porsche's prestigious racing career, and numerous prototype cars. Every aspect of the display was incredible, from cut-away 911s to the huge wall of every car Porsche had ever made, one stacked on the other in chronological order. This was truly the ultimate "car cave."

Yet it was all lost on me. I whined to Wiker. "What the hell does BMW think they're doing? Don't they see this will kill everything? How are we going to keep the factory going? You do realize we'll lose the engineers and most of the maintenance crew in weeks. Then I can't run the factory." Wiker said nothing as I rambled on. He simply focused on the displays with a slight smile, his hands held casually behind his back.

Finally we reached the third floor, at the top of the spiral path. There we saw five pristine 911s—lined up all from different eras and on perfectly lit rotating bases. At first Wiker stood in front of the display and watched each car spin independently. Then he stepped onto one of the bases and rotated along with the car. I stayed by his side, continuing to complain and hounding him for a way forward. He got a whiff of sizzling steak from the adjoining restaurant, and his focus shifted.

He started heading straight to the entrance of the steakhouse, but then he stopped, turned to me, and said in his usual steady voice, "You know, Roger, I find real entrepreneurs always have a plan B. That's how you can tell they're genuine."

Ouch. Was I pretending to be an entrepreneur, or was he just challenging me? Whatever it was, I took the challenge. My mind began to blur with ideas. I knew I had to land on something there and then.

As I looked at the cars, each on their own turntable, my mind stopped spinning, and the plan came to me like a flash through fog. Not everyone had to win. I could choose the winners. It would be costly to me personally, but I could focus the fight away from Farsund. I didn't need to play fair anymore. I could use my enemies' arrogance as a weapon, just as I'd done when Dad's management team tried to topple his company. I could manipulate that vulnerability to Farsund's advantage. I just needed to exploit their own fierce rivalries, leading them to the brink of mutually assured destruction.

The timeline of my plan began to unfold clearly before me. I could see what had to be done, what the risks were, and how I could overcome them. I could make this work, but we only had a handful of days. It would be tricky, and I would burn so many bridges.

The first task—and my only chance—would be to make sure that Wiker bought in.

The delicious aroma of freshly seared steak pulled us into the restaurant. It looked sleek and elegant inside: subdued lighting, white linen draping every table, cutlery perfectly positioned around each pyramid-shaped napkin, dark red carpets matching the window drapes. The maître d' ushered us to a four-setting table and then handed us two menus and a wine list. Each had the iconic 911 profile set in gold against the black background.

I wanted to do nothing but talk Wiker through the plan. I wanted him to say, "There, I knew you were an entrepreneur, and I support you fully." But he didn't. He wouldn't even listen. Burying his head in the menu, it was obvious his mind was set on one thing—steak.

That was one of the most difficult meals I have ever endured. I didn't want to eat. I wanted to get on the phone and get things moving. Time was critical, so I ordered the smallest steak I could find on the menu. Unfortunately it was called a "ladies steak." Even more unfortunately, Wiker noticed and proceeded to chide me for the next forty-five minutes.

Our steaks arrived, precisely positioned on our plates with some freshly seared vegetables. Wiker's portion was huge, about three times the size of mine. We gathered our weapons and stabbed our beasts. The meat was succulent and tender, seared on the outside at 500 degrees but still dark red inside. Back in England, everything was cooked to death. Or boiled. Only when I started traveling around the world did I realize cooking could be an art with a combination of taste, smell, touch, and sensation. And this was one of the best examples.

But I choked on my first bite despite its perfection. I was trying to talk and eat at the same time. My tongue and teeth competed with each other. Finally my teeth won, and I swallowed my first mouthful. "It's all about the…"

Wiker cut me off.

"How's your lady meal? Embrace your feminine side."

"Funny man, ha!" I retorted.

As a teenager I learned about Samuel Taylor Coleridge in school, specifically a story about a drug-induced dream he had. The dream had spun a magical, mythical world that opened itself verse after verse in front of him. Upon awakening, he wanted to do nothing more than write his dream down. Unfortunately he first had to meet with a colleague. Despite his insistence on ending the meeting, it carried on for more than an hour. All but a fraction of his dream had vanished by the time he could put pen to paper. The fragment that remained still became one of the most famous poems of all time: *Kubla Khan*.

What if that happened to me? What if I let this meal drag on? I didn't want to forget my plan. I wanted to share it; to make it real.

Desperate, I tried again. "Do you think the bank…"

It didn't work. He cut me off once more.

"I think Karin could give you fashion advice," he chortled. "Her shoes would suit you."

I figured if I ate quickly, it would encourage him to speed up too. So I cut away as fast as I could at my diminishing steak. Each mouthful received just the necessary number of chews until I was able to swallow. The vegetables took longer, especially the broccoli—crunch, crunch, crunch. I looked like a chipmunk.

Finally my plate was clean. *Had it worked? Had I sped up Wiker's intake?*

No. Wiker chomped away methodically, like a metronome—tick tock.

He glanced at my empty plate. Between bites he said, "It looks like someone was hungry after all. Would you like some of my steak?" Wiker's eyes were smiling, but he remained focused on his next mouthful.

I gave in. He wouldn't be pushed. He had told me what he was going to do. And that's what he did. I sat still, biting my tongue, like a dog begging for attention and waiting in silence.

Eventually, Wiker put down his knife and fork. His plate was empty, his belly was full, his mind was clear, and I now had his undivided attention. He knew I would need it.

"Now, Mr. Cockroft, I'm listening."

CHAPTER 11

The Plan

———

MAY 5, 2009

"How are you going to get BMW to play?" Wiker asked.

"Grab them by the balls and run hard," I replied. "I'm going to war with the whole damn lot of them. It'll be brutal. They fight hard, but there's a chance I could win. It's a tiny, slim chance. That's all we've got."

Now Wiker was listening, I could expand.

"It's actually quite simple. Next year BMW won't need us. They're going to launch a new model five and seven series— new parts, new supplier. But they need us now, for about another six months."

I continued, "There's no way they can get a new supplier to make old parts. We're the only ones that make those parts. That makes me a real threat. I can starve them of parts. They could lose about eighty thousand cars if they don't do what I say. If I'm hard enough, I can make them do anything I want.

I can get them back. Force them into giving us new contracts. Bring back orders they took from us."

"You understand what this will do to you?" Wiker asked.

I did. I knew I'd become their enemy. They were a huge, sophisticated, global organization with endless resources, not someone to pick a fight with. But I had no other choice. This was the right thing to do and the only way I could save the factory, help my friends, and protect Farsund. I'd be a failure if I didn't stand up for the little guy; if I let the bully win.

I would be BMW's villain, not the factory and not Farsund. If I was lucky, this would only destroy my reputation and end my career in the automotive industry. It could get way uglier though. They could sue me or find another way to end me.

"Oh, I'm sure I'll be fine," I said casually.

"How does this affect Porsche and Ferrari?" Wiker knew just what to ask.

"I'm going to screw them just as hard."

I could weaponize Porsche. Solbach would devote the entire might of BMW to fighting against me. He'd lie about those long-term orders I needed. He'd sign any contract, just to get what he wanted. Then he'd break his promises and ditch me and the factory. But he couldn't lie to Porsche. They wouldn't let him. Porsche needed this factory to operate for years. Roth would make Solbach honor BMW's word.

The prospect was intimidating: one man against BMW, Porsche, and Ferrari. Even amid the financial crisis, they had a combined annual revenue of $90 billion. They'd always made it abundantly clear if anyone dared to slap them, they would shoot back, and they were good marksmen. But I set that thought aside and continued to explain my plan. Time was critical. Wiker had to understand every step. I needed his approval.

"This is something only I can do. You can't do it. The old company still has contracts with BMW. This'll be too messy for you. A legal nightmare. But I can. I can set up a new company. I can buy the machines from you. I can do what I like with them, even turn them off. I've got no contracts with any customer. I'll have them by the balls."

Wiker looked fully engaged, but all he said was, "The bank—they need to bless this plan."

The bank still had liens on all the assets, unpaid invoices, and parts manufactured before the bankruptcy. Liens are like mortgages on a house. You own the house, but the bank has a say. If you sell the house, the bank gets paid out first. If you don't pay your mortgage, then the bank can take your house from you. I needed the bank in on this deal. I'd get their support if I persuaded BMW to pay the bank everything they owed and bought all the old parts too. I could get the bank to give my new company a new loan to buy the machines. This was critical: If I owned the machines, the auto giants couldn't buy them, and I could keep them turned off as a form of pressure. But I was running out of time. Wiker's total control expired at the end of July. I had to get BMW to pay those invoices quickly to keep the bank happy while I still had Wiker's authority.

I continued pulling him in. "You can't play football without the ball. I'll set up a company and buy the assets. I'll stop shipping anything to BMW or anyone else. We'll starve them of parts."

Wiker looked at me intently. He was checking every detail in his mind to ensure the plan didn't cross any legal boundaries.

"They have to pay the bank for all the overdue bills. That's the only way I'll start shipping parts again."

"I can imagine the bank will love it," Wiker said with a grin.

"Then I want you to dissolve the bankruptcy agreement you set up back in February. Tell them you're going to close the company. I need to make them scramble. You've got a very credible excuse. We are in real danger of losing our key staff. We won't be able to operate the equipment. We won't be able to make any more parts," I said.

I looked at the empty plates on our table. How appropriate: now dirty dishes, no longer loaded with enticing edibles. But after hot water and a good wash, they'd be gleaming and refreshed. I continued, "You told me you'd only keep the company operating if there was a credible plan to save it. With what BMW just did, it's fair to say our recovery plan is far from credible. There's no reason to operate the company anymore."

This was becoming a high-stakes play. Wiker did not interrupt as I pieced together the plan. "At the same time, you tell them the only way to continue operations until the end of July is for all three—Porsche, Ferrari, and BMW—to pay you a small fortune. I'll work out the details but something like $20 million, enough to pay every employee a bonus for being dragged through this mess.

"Then I'll give them a counteroffer. I'll ask for a big number, but slightly smaller than yours. I doubt they'll take it, but this is where I tell them I own the assets. That should shake them up and really get their attention. It's going to cost them millions, but they'll see it's a drop in the ocean compared to what they could lose if they don't come back to the table," I concluded.

This made Wiker grin again. "I guess Porsche won't like this too much," he chuckled.

My plan hit all three of his objectives: The creditors did well, the employees would do well, and the community would be stronger. As we got up from the table, Wiker implicitly voiced his approval. "Let me call Alan at Landsbanki and set up a meeting."

Early the next morning, Wiker did as he'd promised. "I spoke with Landsbanki, and Alan likes the plan. I'll start to draft up the agreement. Can you be here tomorrow? We can thrash through most of this."

Finally I felt like I could breathe. *This is working. We're doing this. This is huge.* Full of hope, I headed to Oslo.

It took us five days to prepare the contracts. I set up the new company, Buhive A.S., although I had to wait for the government to formally establish a legal entity, which would take about a week. Buhive is an anagram of the first two letters of my three children. VI from Victoria, BE from Benjamin, and HU from Hugo. The name always reminded me of my children. It provided some comfort and made me feel like I was with them.

Contract drafts flew back and forth as we hammered out the specifics of the deal. In little time, we reached an agreement on the most complex points. We only needed to sign now. Alan set up the meeting for Friday, May 15, in the London offices of Landsbanki. Both Wiker and I would be there.

On May 14, the day before my meeting with Landsbanki, Porsche visited the factory again. The trio—Roth, Degler, and Spreiter—were still expecting me to give them a solution.

"Come on, Mr. Cockroft. You must have considered many options. What's your plan? How are you going to get us out of this?" Roth seemed pompous and arrogant. He was taunting me.

I couldn't tell them the actual plan. They'd go crazy. So I said, "I'm working on it. But bloody hell, you're no help at all. Prove you care. I've sent you a bunch of quotes for new business. Give me a new order." I feigned desperation. "Or are you too weak?"

Spreiter took the bait. "Right. I'll do it straight away," he said with a hint of defiance. I'd pushed him into a crazy move: Give a bankrupt company, on the verge of collapse, a new contract for a new car? It sounded crazy, but it sent a very strong message.

Thirty minutes later a fax came through confirming we had been awarded a contract for two parts on the new 911 to be launched in 2011. This was the news I needed, the morale boost that would maintain hope among the employees.

The mood of our meeting lightened toward the end of the day. The Porsche team began to let their guard down. Enthusiastically, I told them, "My plans are almost ready. I'll have them ready next week. First I want to make sure the bank doesn't do anything stupid. I'll go to London and secure the assets."

I'm pretty sure they didn't think through the consequences of what I said at that point though. They didn't know what they were walking into. I didn't like deceiving them, but I was convinced it was the only way this would end successfully.

On May 15, Wiker and I sat in the London offices of Landsbanki as we finalized the deal. Alan and his lawyer team reiterated they wanted me and Wiker to support their effort to recover the late payments from BMW.

"You must stop all shipments until BMW has paid up, and you are not allowed to use the machines to produce any further parts for BMW until they have paid in full. Make them buy all our parts too. I don't want car parts. I want cash," Alan said.

He insisted BMW buy and pay for every part made before bankruptcy too. I could agree to that. Once Alan was happy, once he'd gotten his cash, he would be out of the picture. I didn't need him and wanted him gone.

Alan looked excited. He'd faced a huge loss, but now I'd given him a way to win. "If you do all that, if you get me my money, I'll let you buy the machines for $2 million. Heck, I'll even give you a loan to buy them."

The term of the loan was exactly one year from the first payment, June 30, 2010. I was personally on the hook for $2 million if this went wrong. I would be bankrupt if I failed.

But one year was enough for me to make it work. I urged Landsbanki to sign the contracts at the meeting, but their lawyer insisted they needed one more turn of the paperwork. They promised they would sign them on Monday. A dark cloud—it felt like something was happening behind my back.

Wiker was satisfied, though. He formally agreed to sell me the assets. But only if I used them; only if I saved the factory. If I failed, if I somehow sold the machines for cash, he'd give half straight into the bankrupt estate. That covered his motivation by making it publicly visible.

I wanted a piece of paper proving we'd reached this agreement. I wanted a binding letter of intent. A contract. Wiker then uttered another of his golden comments.

He simply said, "I say what I think, and I do what I say. That should be enough." Great words from a great man—the Norwegian standard.

CHAPTER 12

The Russ

——

MAY 17, 2009

"I bet you can't hang upside down from that branch and drink a shot of aquavit and keep your hat on."

I had to take a look.

It was 2:00 a.m. on the morning of May 17, the final night of the Russ. Eight teenagers milled outside my apartment, all in red dungarees and wearing the signature peaked red cap. One of them was hanging from a tree, downing a shot and, amazingly, still keeping her cap firmly in place. I suspected this wasn't the first shot of the night.

The Russ was a rite-of-passage for any Norwegian teenager celebrating the end of thirteen years of school, the official end of their childhoods. Between May 1 and May 17, all these eighteen-year-old students get to goof around, challenging each other to do dumb stuff. Each time they rise to a challenge, they are rewarded with a badge pin to add to their hats. Somehow Farsund always enjoys great weather for these two weeks, with long and sunny days. But once the Russ is over, teens have to get back to finishing school and take their final exams in June.

The Russ also serves as a prelude to the Norwegian National Constitution Day. On this day in 1814, Norway signed its constitution, gained independence from Denmark, and entered into a union with Sweden. The two countries shared a Swedish king up until 1905, when they finally dissolved their union and became independent countries. For Norwegians, this historic moment represents one of the biggest celebrations of the year.

On National Day, the communities of each town come together and share their time. Neighbors assemble a potluck breakfast of smoked salmon, scrambled eggs, and champagne. The festivities and Norwegian fare continue throughout the day. Children get the rare opportunity to eat their own body weight in hotdogs and ice cream. So many parties dot the town that people can simply roll from one to the next. Doors stay open. Everyone is welcome.

The most important part of the day centers on the parade. Norway has strict rules regarding their national flag. It can't be raised before 8:00 a.m. and must be lowered by 8:00 p.m. But decorations can be hung in advance, so in the week before, these can be seen brightening the windows of every home, street, and lamp post. Then at exactly 8:00 a.m. on National Day, flags are raised on every single flagpole.

The townspeople proudly don the bunad, a traditional costume based on one's town of birth. Women wear a full-length skirt, usually black, a white blouse with a fancy collar, and a red or black waistcoat adorned with detailed brass buttons, silver trinkets, and embroidered patterns. Men wear a green waistcoat and black jacket, also with brass buttons, over a white shirt. Three-quarter length dark pants fit tightly just below the knees, paired with white, full-length socks and buckled shoes. Everyone sports a ribbon in dazzling red, white, and blue. The trinkets, patterns, and detailed embroidery all symbolize something. Wearing these costumes is a sign of respect and pride for one's community and heritage.

The procession starts around 11:00 a.m., beginning at the central school. The sidewalks are packed with townspeople cheering and waving flags. Following a marching band, led by girls impressively twirling their batons, the youngest children parade through the streets wearing pink caps. As the children's contingent snakes its way up and down the streets, it grows larger in size. Each class adds itself successively to the end of the line. The one exception is the Russ year. This is the teens' last chance to ape around. They dart in and out of the procession, trying to cause confusion and mayhem, completing their final challenges and collecting the last pins.

No one works on National Day, not even Wiker. So I decided to take the morning off and join the crowd of spectators outside my apartment. I put on a suit and tie, added the national ribbon to my lapel, and off I went. As I examined the crowd, the first thought that crossed my mind was, *This is real.* I knew many people from work, but until now I didn't know who their partners, children, or parents were. Here today, everyone had gathered outside, eagerly waiting for the parade. Large groups of friends and families meandered through the streets and merged with other groups. I almost felt as if I belonged.

As I crossed the street, people came up to me, shook my hand, and uttered, "Gratulerer i dag (Congratulations today)." At first, I figured this was simply what you did on National Day. But the strange thing was I didn't really recognize these people, even though they seemed to know me. "Cockroft, you're a good man," said one stranger, and I heard variations of this many times. Soon I was surrounded by people patting me on the shoulder or shaking my hand.

Then the mayor of the community, Stein Ytterdahl, barged through the crowd wearing his mayoral chains. "There he is," Ytterdahl boomed. "There's our fighter!" He grabbed my hand and shook it vigorously as he put his other hand on my arm.

I'd already passed through the doors of Farsund's community. The mayor was telling me. The people were showing me. I belonged. This was one of the most important and touching moments of my life. The factory held special importance for every member of the community. All knew a fierce battle was raging, and they trusted me as their fighter. I no longer felt invisible. Farsund had become part of me. My new home.

PART 2

CASTING

CHAPTER 13

The Dark Demons

———

It's easy to become devoted to the international brands that German car makers have created: BMW, Porsche, VW, Mercedes-Benz, and Audi. People associate themselves with what the brand stands for: power, prestige, elegance, sophistication. All desirable qualities; the public face these companies want you to see.

The strength of each brand didn't happen by chance. It was forged by the power these auto giants wield, behind the scenes and hidden from view—hidden because they act with utmost ruthlessness, doing whatever it takes to achieve their primary goal of dominating the market. They all compete for this market—the global luxury market, the most profitable of all. In 2021 alone, luxury auto sales totaled more than $540 billion.[1]

Demonstrations of dominance are critical to survive this competition. Each company has staked out a city to signify their empire: Munich for BMW, Ingolstadt for Audi, Wolfsburg for VW, and Stuttgart for Porsche and Mercedes-Benz. They mark their territories with gargantuan structures, headquarters, museums, racetracks, and even so-called "experience centers."

Every symbolic display costs billions in a mounting battle to outshine the other.

Dramatic power plays are commonplace, inherent to the game itself. In 1959, Mercedes-Benz nearly took over BMW, and it was only through the efforts of BMW's chairman, Herbert Quandt, and a government bail-out that BMW could wriggle off the hook.[2] Nearly four decades later, in 1998, BMW turned around and became the predator, going toe-to-toe against VW in an attempt to buy Rolls-Royce. VW believed it had won after buying the aging Rolls-Royce factory and the lesser Bentley brand, but BMW proceeded to steal the Rolls-Royce brand right from under VW's nose.[3]

Then in 2009, Wendelin Wiedeking, the CEO of Porsche, made one of the largest power plays ever seen. His ambitious plan to use Porsche to take over the much larger VW nearly succeeded. Wiedeking was accused of breaking a slew of laws and never informed the markets of his takeover intentions. Some investors lost millions, and one committed suicide. In the eleventh hour, Ferdinand Piëch, chairman of VW and grandson of Ferdinand Porsche, managed to thwart Wiedeking and push for his replacement.[4] The fierce feud that ensued reflected how many powerful families are interspersed throughout the German automotive industry. The Quandt, Klatten, Piëch, and Porsche families collectively own BMW, VW, Porsche, Rolls-Royce, Bentley, Mini, Audi, Lamborghini, Seat, Skoda, and Ducati.

In this world, then, vested interests abound, fueling the countless lies that prop up their system. For instance, between 2009 and 2014, these automakers conspired to make the electronics on their diesel cars hide the amount of harmful emissions generated. Lawmakers cracked down, fining VW billions. It wasn't just them. BMW was fined $442 million. Mercedes-Benz got fined too but managed to dodge their $880 million penalty by ratting the others out. In the end VW estimated it cost them more than $31 billion.[5,6,7,8,9,10]

The companies clearly don't trust one another, but they will sometimes work together when they sense an individual benefit. Regardless of antitrust laws, these brands will pool their resources and share information when they deem it absolutely necessary. They recognize that between them, they manufacture nearly six million cars each year domestically and another 5.5 million overseas.[11] Together, they carry a very big stick, one that will crush anyone who gets in their way or disrespects the pecking order.

Like any monopoly, those at the top reap boundless rewards for maintaining supremacy. Dr. Herbert Diess, once head of BMW's supply chain and later as Chairman of VW, enjoyed an annual paycheck of more than $11 million. Before being ousted from VW in 2022, he lived like a king, with private jets, prestige autos, and luxurious amenities wherever he went. He lorded over 660,000 employees scattered around the globe.[12] And he wasn't the only one. Each auto empire has the exact same type of king at their helm.

The allure of this glitzy lifestyle cascades down each organization, reaching even the lowest rungs. Every single employee either hides or desperately fights to climb that greasy career pole, determined to achieve greater status and to wield their own power inside and outside the organization.

Motivated by fear, they have an unwavering commitment to defending their territory, their leader, and, most importantly, their beloved brand. Get something wrong, and they face a fate worse than death—a window job.

To be a vendor, to supply parts, you have to understand and respect this intricate world. The German auto giants prefer vendors called Mittelstand companies, family-owned businesses often bound by friendship or even blood to the super auto families. They started small years ago and grew along with their customers, sometimes to massive heights. Benteler, Georg Fischer, Robert Bosch, Kostal, Hülsbeck & Fürst—the list is endless. Like the auto giants, these vendors claim dominance in their own town or city, functioning as their customers' dedicated police force. They will do whatever they're told, not bound by public scrutiny. In return for their compliance, they get business.

What unifies those at the top with those at the bottom, besides a fanatical devotion to their brand? A threat from the outside. That threat will galvanize the generals, captains, and foot soldiers into one cohesive killing machine. They will use all their collective resources and capabilities to thwart it. And who decides what counts as a threat? Those who have the cunning and cleverness to use this machine to its fullest.

Frank Solbach and Martin Roth knew exactly how to do that.

CHAPTER 14

Five Bombs

MAY 18 TO 25, 2009

"I don't have a plan B," she said.

Kristen Ommundsen was one of our finest mechanical engineers, a graduate from Trondheim's Norwegian University of Science and Technology. That distinction didn't keep her from going into the trenches, though. She was the one who voluntarily cleaned all the bathrooms in the days before bankruptcy when we couldn't pay our housekeeping vendor. Farsund meant everything to her.

That morning, May 18, Kristen approached me after the daily production meeting and factory walk-around. She opened up, echoing what I had heard from Hilde and so many others. "I have three children at home. I'm a single parent, and my mum looks after my kids during the day. I can't live anywhere else but here."

As she begged me to do my best, I felt overcome with a new feeling—determination. Families were at risk, the community would suffer, and the factory could close. All because of the blind-sighted arrogance of these auto giants.

BOMB NUMBER ONE

My determination fueled me in the difficult days ahead. I worked furiously in my office with my team while Wiker and his team did the same from Oslo. My plan had many moving parts, and I needed to ensure they were all coordinated across five discrete stages. I could leave nothing to chance.

First, I went to the office of Dr. Jan Ove Loland. He worked with our customers' technical teams and invented all the new tools. Jan Ove looked like a nutty professor who was always dressed impeccably. Yet he had no idea about fashion. He didn't care how he looked at all. His mind was focused solely on solving technical problems. His wife picked out his clothes every morning and laid them on his bed.

Jan Ove had snuck out a prototype tool to the team at Mercedes when the factory went bankrupt in January. It meant we had nothing to negotiate with Mercedes. It was probably the right decision, but I couldn't let him do that again with Porsche or BMW. "Things are going to get ugly," I told him with urgency. "We have to stay together, as a team— one unit. Understand?"

"Yes, I support you," he replied, but it didn't sound as if he meant it. He sounded more like he was about to tell me what he would prefer to do. I didn't allow him the opportunity.

"Don't even think about talking to anyone. Do nothing. No response to any customer. Just tell me everything you hear." I tried to stay calm, but there was angst in my voice.

"But, well, maybe I could…" I cut him off.

"We're on a knife's edge. You could kill this company if you pull another one of your January stunts." He knew exactly what I was referring to. "Not a single thing. Please, I need it all. Promise me?"

"I get it. I promise. I won't talk to anyone." He was desperate. This job was his technical paradise, and he would do nothing to hurt it.

Next I headed to Rune Almas's office. He ran the factory on a daily basis and knew how to turn the machines on and off.

"I'm going to ask you to do something very odd. I'm going to ask you to stop all production later today. I don't want anything shipped out either. Close the doors. Nothing goes until I say." He looked intrigued but didn't press for an explanation.

"Okay. I'll find things for my team to do. How long do you think this will last?" he asked.

"We'll know in a week," I replied firmly. I knew it would be an excruciating wait, but it was the only way.

Finally, I went onto the factory floor to see Einar Johansen, the best tooling manager I've ever worked with.

"This is going to sound weird. But imagine someone came in to grab our tools. How could you make sure they couldn't use them? What pieces would you take and, I don't know, say… hide?" I tried to sound casual, but Einar could sense the collusion.

"Oh, I could think of one or two valves. That would do it. Maybe a slider or two." Einar smiled. He was on board too.

"Get ready to do it with all BMW tools tomorrow." I winked and went back to my office.

Around 9:00 p.m. that evening, everything had been prepared. I was ready to unleash a series of bombs designed to shock, confuse, and surprise the other side. Wiker had double checked the legal ramifications. We were now on the phone together, teetering on the edge of a precipice.

"One last opportunity, Håvard. Once we press the button, we can't go back. They will retaliate very hard, from every direction. They might even win. Are you really ready to do this?" I had to give him the opportunity to back out, even though I sincerely hoped he wouldn't.

"Let me think about it for a moment." Then, silence. He'd ended our call.

The world felt as if it had stopped spinning, as if time had slowed to a snail's pace. I kept staring at the clock. Every second ticked past in slow motion. Then, after twenty excruciating minutes, an email popped up in my inbox.

Wiker had done it. He'd pressed the button. The war had started. But it wasn't just a war of us against them. We were also trying to incite a destructive internal squabble, one that would be costly to recover from. He'd emailed all of them—Solbach, Roth, Vezzani—and terminated his agreement. He gave them until May 27, just nine more days, until the doors of the factory shut. He spat out a laundry list of legal reasons for the termination, with BMW being the primary one. Solbach's directive to cut orders at the end of April left no credible future for the factory, Wiker wrote.

He gave them only one option to avoid their impending demise: They could send him $26 million within those nine days. A large chunk of that sum would go toward incentivizing the employees to stay. This was our way of rubbing salt into a newly made gash.

Then came the final punch: Wiker demanded BMW pay their outstanding bills to the bank. No parts would be shipped to any of them until BMW paid their dues.

He had timed his message to hit at the end of the day when they had let their guard down; timed to deprive them of restful sleep. Closing the factory gifted each of them with their own specific nightmare.

For BMW, this meant they would not have the parts to make eighty thousand E6X cars, the last build before they released a new model. They would face an estimated loss of about $3.2 billion over a six-month period.

For Porsche, this meant the Panamera would be delayed for three years while they searched for another supplier. They would face an estimated loss of about $3.3 billion in sales spread over three years.

For Ferrari, this meant they would have to find another supplier and not be able to produce any cars for at least two years. They would face an estimated loss of about $1.6 billion. They would not have survived.

If we shut down, so might they. Did they think they were too big to fail? By fighting back, Farsund was showing them, in fact, they were too big to think.

At BMW, Solbach had to call his boss, Joachim Goldbach, and explain just how he had wound up in this position. In turn, Goldbach had to take this to Philip-Christian Eller and Dr. Herbert Diess, both senior board members of BMW.

Ben Bernanke, then chairman of the US Federal Reserve, was clear that the "lack of credit" caused companies to fail.[1] Analysts had predicted BMW would run out of cash around June 2009.[2] Farsund would just make it worse—much worse.

At Porsche, Roth and Spreiter had to inform the CEO Wendelin Wiedeking and Wiedeking's finance chief Holger Härter. Wiedeking was in the midst of his audacious power play to take over the entire VW empire, fending off attacks from vested families, shareholders, and governments. He knew he'd look like a fool if he didn't launch his new car, especially for such a trivial issue Farsund represented.

Everything hung in the balance now, but one thing was certain. Farsund, a small Norwegian town, had landed squarely on the radars of the most senior executives at BMW, Porsche, and Ferrari.

BOMB NUMBER TWO

On the authority of Wiker and with the express insistence of Alan, the Landsbanki banker, I stopped all shipments to the big three automakers. Now I was starving them of parts. Their in-house supplies would run dry very soon. No more parts would be sent until they paid the arrears to Landsbanki.

All our machines stopped. Jan Ove didn't sneak any tools back to our customers. He didn't even speak to them. Rune Almas made sure our team focused on maintenance and housekeeping. Einar Johansen dismantled the BMW tools and molds. We wanted the automakers to panic. I knew they'd fight back fiercely, but I had to think five steps ahead and consider every possible scenario. Things would unfold quickly, and I had no time to pause.

The most critical issue at this point was the assets, or the "football," as I liked to call them. I still didn't have anything in writing confirming I owned them. Night was creeping in, but I stayed glued to my office phone, pestering Wiker for the letter spelling out my ownership. He repeatedly asked why I thought I'd need it.

"My word is my bond. Is that not enough for you?"

"Håvard, we've just cut them off and demanded $26 million or risk losing billions of dollars. You know they're coming for us, don't you? They're going to fight. They will definitely use this. Expect the extreme. I trust you. I don't trust them."

Late that night, Wiker managed to get me a contract signed by him but not by Landsbanki. I finally had some proof I owned the football.

The following day, May 19, Buhive A.S. was formally associated just in the nick of time. I took possession of all the machinery, furniture, computers, vehicles—everything except the cast parts. I had signed an agreement with Wiker that the bankrupt estate could continue to use the equipment to honor Wiker's commitments. This meant he had authority to negotiate with the automakers.

Wiker flew down from Oslo that same morning. Our team had to know what was happening and what we were risking. Two hundred people gathered in the canteen area again.

I cleared my throat and started to speak, "You all know what BMW did at the meeting in Munich." I looked at the floor and shook my head. I still couldn't fathom why they had done what they had. "It means any hope of raising an investment fund is dead. We can't get investors if we don't have a real business plan." Everyone let out a collective sigh.

Then I said, "This is where I'm going to take my gloves off. Fight dirty, and fight hard." Cheers erupted.

"Mr. Wiker," I turned and pointed him out, "has sold me all the equipment: every single machine, every spare part, even the conveyors—everything." The room went quiet as they awaited an explanation.

"They still need us. I'm going to starve them out. Make them bleed until they beg us to make parts for them again." Silence gave way to laughs and cries of amazement.

"We've demanded they pay us $26 million to keep production alive until the end of July. I've told them they don't get a single part until we get the cash. Not Ferrari, not Porsche, and especially not BMW. They get nothing."

Over thunderous applause, I continued, "If this works, you should all receive a sizable chunk of change as a bonus." This was the point of my entire fight. I wanted to make everyone around me a winner. I wasn't going to sit by and watch them get screwed by greedy auto giants. Of course I was grabbing this bull by the balls. You're all in once you do that.

Wiker stepped in next to explain he had terminated the contract with the automakers and therefore had to put everyone on a one-week termination of employment notice. BMW needed to understand this represented a real threat. We could only do this by bringing the factory cogs to a grinding halt.

I had a few last words of reassurance. "If our plan doesn't work, the factory will close, and we are all out of a job. We are reaching the end game. We will fight to the very end

with anything we can. The only way to win is to go all in."
Everyone roared and applauded vigorously.

As the team dispersed, Helge Fait, the HR director, came up
to me and said, "Incredible. You sack every single one of us,
yet they applaud you?" He wandered off, looking perplexed.

Later that day, trucks turned up at the factory door looking
for parts, a sign of BMW refusing to believe we'd cut them
off. A standoff ensued. First a truck from Regensburg showed
up, then one from Oxford, then another from Dingolfing,
and then a couple more from Regensburg. Soon the empty
parking lot was completely filled with trucks, all waiting in
line for days outside the plant. They got nothing.

BOMB NUMBER THREE

Night fell. May 19, I sent the next shock, timed exactly twenty-
four hours after Wiker's email. I told the automakers I now
owned the assets, and I offered the exact same deal as Wiker—
except for the price. It would only cost them $23 million,
about $3 million cheaper than his offer. The message couldn't
have been clearer: *I have the football, and I'm going to play
hard.* Reality was trumping arrogant entitlement in Munich
and Stuttgart.

The German contingent went into a tailspin. BMW started
to organize what they called "private customer support
meetings" at the FIZ in Munich. They insisted these meetings
be held in Munich because of the unspoken pecking order:
BMW was the largest of the three automakers, so they had

the right to summon Porsche and Ferrari to their offices. It was obvious they weren't a team even as they planned their counterattack.

Meanwhile, Wiker and I refused to answer the barrage of questions coming from BMW and Porsche. Only the Ferrari representative, Luca Vezzani, didn't ask a single thing.

For the next few days, Wiker and I were told to join multiple conference calls to explain our plan. They wanted breakdowns of how we would use the money and what alternatives existed. Wiker had no reason or need to explain himself. As the administrator, he was fully authorized to act autonomously. So we just ignored them.

BOMB NUMBER FOUR

Ferrari and two of the biggest German automakers were now starved of parts and facing a choice between a total shutdown or two expensive, humiliating counteroffers. Now that we had their undivided attention, it was time to start the countdown and run fast.

Wiker's next email got them scrambling. He reminded them the factory would close in just a few more days. He reminded them nothing got shipped until BMW paid its debts. He reminded them I owned the equipment. Then he informed them he knew of my counter offer, and he endorsed it. He confirmed they had just those three options—nothing else.

He finished by dismissing their persistent demands to meet:

It is not of interest for the bankruptcy estate to travel to Munich for an afternoon meeting with the agenda to discuss options and final agreement. The options are presented.

If you would like to meet with me, you are of course free to come to Oslo. However, I think a meeting without Mr. Cockroft is of no value at the moment, and any meeting will need to have an agenda with proposals to be dealt with.

They had no way out except the one we dictated. I don't think anything could have infuriated them more.

BOMB NUMBER FIVE

Rumors of what we were doing spread like wildfire throughout the industry. I'd even been approached by one of the representatives from Alcoa, Martin Vos, who wanted to hear the story firsthand. On Monday, May 25, we were sitting at a meeting table in my office when Elizabeth, the receptionist, suddenly burst into the room.

"It's Mr. Roth and Mr. Solbach on the phone. They insist they speak to you."

The "dream team," as I now facetiously called them, had again assembled in the FIZ. I'd had a number of calls that morning on both my cell and landline, but I'd ignored them. Apologizing to my guest, I picked up the phone this time. Vos decided to stay and listen to what I'm sure was one of the most intense business calls he'd ever heard.

"Ah, Mr. Cockroft! I'm so glad you found time to take this call," said Solbach, with his usual patronizing tone. "Representatives from Porsche and Ferrari are with me in Munich. We have decided to accept your offer, Mr. Cockroft. We will pay you $23 million to secure production for June and July."

I was surprised. He'd stunned me. What was he trying to do? He continued, "But the factory will be closed sometime after that. I want you to promise us you'll be cooperative, work with us, play nice, as we move our orders elsewhere..."

Did Solbach believe I would simply watch as they slowly killed Farsund? That I would be a spectator to a terrible act? Did they assume I'd sell my soul and be blinded by greed?

I interrupted him and said, "I don't think you understand."

This was it. I was about to show BMW and Porsche who their true enemy was. I was about to kill any future I might have in the automotive industry.

I took a deep breath and uttered the words that changed everything: "I can promise you it will cost you $40 million for every month you need to use my equipment. I know you have the power to close this company down, but you need us for at least six more months. So, I'll make sure when you do kill us, everyone in Farsund will be a millionaire." I hung up the phone.

Later Martin Roth and Karin Degler told me how my message was received in their meeting. They said in the awkward silence that followed the end of our call, Vezzani of Ferrari pushed back from the meeting table in Munich, looked at the BMW contingent, and said, "Gentlemen, Ferrari is out. This is just too expensive," before leaving the meeting room. Roth was clear to me how that had made him feel.

Back in my office, I looked across the table at Martin Vos, who was now white in the face and staring at me with his mouth agape. He could only muster, "I can see you are busy," before gripping my hand and shaking it vigorously. "Good luck."

CHAPTER 15

Mutually Assured Destruction

———

MAY 26 TO 27, 2009

Maybe I can be a fisherman? It could be my new job.

I sat on the edge of the harbor wall, watching a small fleet of three tiny fishing boats return from their daily endeavor. My feet dangled above the sea, waves gently washing against them and making the sandy bottom sparkle. The fresh air helped clear my mind—the perfect end to a turbulent day.

I thought about the tight timeline we faced. Solbach and Roth had less than two days, but they would use it fully. While my threat to starve BMW seemed impenetrable, it was not. Wiker had control of the situation for just two more months, until July. The bank had agreed to let Wiker sell the machines to me. But they hadn't put anything in writing. My plan could go to hell in two months. I'd have no leverage. Someone could steal the factory away from me, run it into the ground, then close it, just like Solbach had threatened. So they had two days to find a way to hold Wiker off for two months.

Just as harrowing, we had exactly enough of the precious parts to keep BMW running for another two months. These were parts the bank insisted BMW buy. They had everything they needed to wait out the reign of Wiker. This was a weakness in my plan. They hadn't seen it yet, but I was sure they would.

None of this was about me. My automotive career was already over because of the stunt I'd pulled earlier that day. I was BMW's enemy. A big army will always defeat a single soldier, eventually. Yet Farsund and my team were the only ones who deserved to win. I just hoped I could hold out long enough for them to get their bright future. The war would be brutal, but there was no way to avoid fighting it.

I sighed and muttered, "Oh well, never mind."

"What do you think?" Wiker's mood was bright, almost amazed.

It was May 26, the day after my phone call with Solbach. Wiker and I had spent most of the morning speculating what would happen next. Now we'd both been copied on an email from Karin Degler of Porsche. The email said both BMW and Porsche had agreed to Wiker's offer. Together, they would pay the $26 million Wiker demanded. Cutting Ferrari out of receiving any parts was their most bitter request, retaliation for Vezzani's insubordination.

"I don't know," I said. "Did you see the attachments they sent?"

Wiker paused as he opened the two attachments. "These are confirmations of payments. That's good. Who are these people that signed them?"

"Interesting. Porsche used their financial controller. They used letterheaded official documents too. Which sort of makes me think it's real." I was scrutinizing every detail closely. "Wow, wait. Do you see who signed the BMW documents?"

"I see the names. Who are they?" Wiker wasn't familiar with everyone in the automotive world.

"These are big guns. Philip Christian Eller, Dr. Johann Wieland, and their rising superstar Dr. Herbert Diess. They're all senior board members. They run most of the company. Bloody hell, they're very big boys." Part of me was impressed. I'd gotten this little issue, a faraway Norwegian town, on their big German desks. But part of me was also suspicious. Somehow this just didn't feel right.

"Congratulations, Mr. Cockroft." Wiker was satisfied. He represented the Norwegian government. He sincerely believed the boards of BMW and Porsche would never dare lie to him.

I didn't have the same confidence. "I think this is a plot. They did this in January, when they promised to pay money until the last moment. They did this at the end of April too. I think they're going to do this again. This is only real when the cash is in our account."

Wiker wanted to believe he could trust BMW's word, but my persistence made him start to wonder. *Could they really be so stupid as to let the factory close?* So he sent another email insisting both Porsche and BMW prove they had transferred the cash, that they had paid all their old bills, and they would buy all the old parts. He warned them again if they didn't, he would close everything tomorrow, May 27, and even cut the power, letting the metal cool off and eventually solidify in the machines.

We heard nothing from either Solbach or Roth for four hours. Then Wiker sent a second, even more urgent email: *"Where's the money?"*

But they continued to bide their time. I could feel the wheels of their plot turning, even though I couldn't hear or see them. After another four hours, well after the banks had closed, Dr. Schleinitz finally responded:

I am sure you must know that bank transactions are done overnight. There is no confirmation of booking before it actually has taken place during the night. We cannot influence that process. Please contact us, when you have got the payments.

I called Wiker again as soon as Schleinitz's message came through and said, "There, they've shown their hand. They waited until the banks closed. Wire transactions don't happen overnight. They only happen when banks are open."

"And why did Schleinitz respond to the email you sent to Solbach?" I answered my own question. "Because they're working on something. He's their lawyer. They're coordinated."

Now we could only wait. We'd find out tomorrow, the day Wiker had set for the potential factory closure. Our phone meeting with the auto giants was scheduled for noon—after when the money should have arrived.

The bank opened on the fateful day at 9:00 a.m. Knut Nesvold, my finance guy, was stationed there, next to the bank manager Johnny, and just as I'd feared: no transaction, no money. Wiker couldn't believe they lied. He scrambled to ask for BMW's and Porsche's help in tracking down the glitch, begging them for transaction numbers or any official documents he could work with. But they remained silent.

Wiker gradually grew more frustrated. Finally, at 11:04 a.m., he fired off one last email, just before the meeting was about to start:

Please respond to my email. We need to know.

I knew their silence was their response, a classic BMW ploy. *Distract your enemy with a promise of the best outcome while you prepare and deliver the worst.* But this time, the third time, I was ready. I'd prepared. If I didn't win, everyone would lose.

Around 11:30 a.m., the usual suspects—Solbach, Hierl, Roth, Degler, and Schleinitz—gathered once again in the FIZ and prepared to deliver their sting. Meanwhile, I sat in my office in Farsund and Wiker in his office in Oslo, both of us awaiting the fateful phone call. Fifteen minutes later, Solbach dropped his first bomb. His foot soldier Reinhold

Hierl sent an email to Wiker, an offer to buy the assets, signed by Solbach and Roth. The email included the bank's lawyer team. The bank, Alan McClaren, had played both us and BMW. I figured that Solbach had found him, wooed him with a promise of money, and got him to flip. Of course he'd offered to pay the bank for all the outstanding bills, even pay off the loan on the equipment. He'd offered all the money the bank wanted. And Alan McClaren bought it: a quick solution to a difficult problem; a promise from BMW for lots of cash.

Solbach was ready for the final attack, savoring his moment in the spotlight. Every board member in BMW had their eyes on him. Even the Porsche CEO, Wendelin Wiedeking, had approved this plan. These lofty senior executives were eagerly waiting to witness the execution of an Englishman. Excitement mounted as noon ticked closer.

But Solbach and Roth were overconfident. Word of their scheme had already leaked out at both BMW and Porsche. It even reached the Porsche design engineering department, where a man named Lutz Bauer worked. Lutz then called one of my guys, Henning Omdal.

In a childish, taunting tone, Lutz said, "We just bought your assets. Now we own you, and you have to turn the machines back on and make our parts."

With two minutes to go, Henning ran into my office to relay this message.

The meeting started as the clock struck noon. Hierl talked first. "Mr. Wiker, we have secured the assets. Landsbanki has agreed to sell them to us." He paused before reading the next sentence of his well-rehearsed script.

"We have agreed to pay all other outstanding amounts too. So the bank will have nothing more to do with Farsund or the bankruptcy estate."

You could hear some murmurs in the background as he continued, "That means the bankruptcy estate is concluded."

His next comment was what they had all been all waiting for. "We have no need for Mr. Cockroft. He can leave."

I sat there silently. Wiker did not. He interrupted Hierl with a single word: "Stop."

The angry side of Wiker had been unleashed. When Wiker got angry, he became very slow and deliberate. His voice deepened and firmed. Extremely firm. He grabbed your attention and didn't let it go until he chose to. It was exactly what I wanted: an angry, defiant, and motivated Håvard Wiker. He had been lied to, both by the automakers and the bank, and he had no tolerance for deception.

"You do not own these assets. I owned them, and I have sold them to Roger. They are not the bank's assets to sell. Because you have reneged on your commitment, I have no alternative but to instruct Mr. Cockroft to close the factory. All contracts will be canceled today."

His booming voice gave way to a deafening silence. He just hung up, ending the meeting. Their plan had failed. My plan had failed too. We each faced mutually assured destruction. They thought they'd outsmarted us. They thought they knew bankruptcy law. They knew the laws in Germany, but not in Norway. Wiker was that expert.

CHAPTER 16

Windfall

MAY 27 TO 28, 2009

Now Wiker held absolute authority and absolute control. He was ready to shut the factory down for good. In our post-meeting call, he told me to inform the staff of the news. He would cancel all contracts by the end of the day. The machines would be terminally ruined once the electricity was shut off.

For Wiker, it was over. But a wise man once told me entrepreneurs always have a plan B. I did.

Make them believe it and create chaos. I had to make sure the automakers panicked. The factory was shutting down permanently. They had to hear it from Wiker, they had to read it in the press, and they had to learn it from the people of Farsund. Only then, on the brink of chaos, would they listen to me.

The complexity of my plan was both its weakness and its strength. Stupid is always the neighbor to brave. One wrong step and Farsund would lose. I'd be a humiliated fool. But if I could spook Solbach and Roth, they'd play it my way. I could get them to pay loads of money—money that would allow me to reward the employees handsomely. In the process, BMW would see the true cost they faced if the factory closed.

Wiker fired the first shot in this new battle by officially rejecting their proposal to take over the factory. His email read:

Your offer is surprising and destructive in regard to a solution for the factory and for BMW and Porsche. It will not be accepted.

I'm very sorry that you have made the wrong decisions.

It got them stirred up. They scrambled to find lawyers who understood Norwegian law.

I gave them time, a couple of hours. The next message would come from my people.

I walked to the canteen to tell my team at exactly 3:00 p.m., trailed by cameras clicking in my face and bright flashes blinding me. The press had already invaded the factory. They knew something big was about to unfold. I made sure to shut the meeting room doors tightly before turning to my team. The entire staff were silent.

"The plan didn't work. BMW and Porsche tried to trick us. They lied. The money never came through."

Those were some of the hardest words I'd ever had to say in my life. And the looks on their faces afterward only made things harder. Every one of them in the packed room stared at me, barely blinking. They hung onto my every word as I continued.

"We took a risk, the only thing we had left to do. We lost." Mouths dropped. Quiet chatter bounced around the room as my words were translated into Norwegian.

"I'm dreadfully sorry. The factory doors will close for good at the end of this meeting. Please gather up your things and go home." I was brutal. I needed the press to capture their reactions.

They had no questions, just shock. People slowly rose and headed back to their usual workplaces to collect their belongings, clear out their desks, and take one last look at where they'd spent so many years and so much effort.

I felt like a failure and a traitor. But I knew some of them would talk to their contacts in Porsche or BMW. Those were the people who had to hear hope no longer existed. It would sound like a genuine message.

It wasn't difficult to get the press to broadcast my story. They craved dramatic news just like this: the disastrous downfall of a factory, a defeated team, a slain warrior. They plastered the news on the internet immediately and on the front page of the next day's paper. I knew the giants were watching.

Before everyone left, I gathered my direct reports into my office and instructed, "Get as many contact numbers as you can. Make sure your phones are on and stand by. I'm going to need you tonight."

Rune looked at me with curiosity, his head slightly tilted, eyes narrowed, the hint of a smile on his face. "So you've got a plan, then? This isn't over yet?"

My reply was simple: "I've got my job to do." Hope filled the room.

It must have been a somber mood in Munich as the automakers realized their scheme had failed and they faced a catastrophic loss of production.

I was on my own in the factory. It felt desolate now everyone else had left for home. The newspaper and TV reporters were also gone, working on this breaking news. Then unexpectedly, someone appeared to fill the emptiness: Hilde, the logistical manager who had once warned me, "Don't fuck this up."

"Just about all of us are going to the bar to drown our sorrows and watch the game." Barcelona was playing against Manchester United in the UEFA Champions League Cup Final. "Everyone wants you there. I want you there. Will you come?" Her invitation gave me such a positive jolt, like electricity.

I still had work to do. "I promise I'll be there for the second half. Save me a pint."

Hilde would have to wait, though. It was 7:00 p.m., and I had to contact Roth to extend an olive branch.

"Martin, how's your day going?" I tried to sound as casual as I could.

"I've had better," he replied.

Reality had settled in at the FIZ and in Stuttgart. Roth knew my call was his last chance to avert disaster. He had to listen. He had to act. I needed him to move fast. I wanted to give him something that would enable him to regain some respect in his organization; make this an easy pill to swallow; coat it in sugar.

"Can I ask where you are?"

Roth answered, "I'm in my garden watering my lawn. It's what I do to relax."

I wasn't sure how to respond. It was hard for me to imagine Martin Roth relaxing, let alone tending to his garden. I'd once looked up his address on the internet and saw pictures of a home that looked like a fortress and certainly not an easy place to relax around.

"I've got an idea. Are you ready to listen?"

I waited silently until he said, "Yes, Roger, I'm listening."

"Let's do half. We cut the cash call to $13 million for one month. You get your side to agree to work on a long-term solution with me for the next thirty days, but we have a hard stop at the end of June."

I waited for Roth to say something, but he remained silent. So I continued, "You pissed Wiker off, but I think I can get him to agree to this. Everything else, all the other conditions, stay the same. The outstanding debt and the inventory must be paid before I can ship anything."

Now Roth interjected, "And you pissed off everyone in BMW. But Wiedeking came to my office this evening. He told me to find a way to solve this. Can we really find a long-term solution in one month?" What he meant was: *Can I really trust you?*

"Yes. We have no other choice," I said.

Roth now grew engaged and eager. "Give me some minutes to call my people and BMW. I must get this signed off from our bosses."

Before letting him go, I pressed my point one more time. "Martin, this is your last chance. No more games. Everyone has been sacked. They will start finding jobs tomorrow. Lose the people, and we don't have a factory. Anyway, the electricity gets cut off tonight. The metal freezes tomorrow morning. No more machines. You've got thirty minutes."

I heard him sigh. "I know," he said briskly.

Our call ended. This was exactly what he needed—a solution he could take to Wiedeking. I didn't want him to fail. I didn't want him replaced. I would need him later.

My next call was to Wiker. At first, he couldn't believe what I had done. "They have told us so many lies today. Why do you believe them now?"

"They have nowhere else to go. It's either this or they lose billions of dollars. I can get this done in a month, Håvard. Give me a chance." Wiker finally relented and revised the offer. After his approval, I sent it over to Roth.

At about 7:30 p.m., Roth got back to me. He spoke in a stilted and unemotional manner, as if this were just a routine call. "The management board of both Porsche and BMW are in agreement with your proposal, Mr. Cockroft. We will wire the money as soon as the banks open in the morning. Expect it in your account before noon. We will send you confirmations from our banks as soon as the wire is complete."

Suddenly, his tone shifted to one of anxiety. "Will you confirm the factory is safe?"

I didn't give him much. "I've agreed with Wiker. The power will stay on, but the employees are still sacked. Get me the money, and I'll try to get the people back."

Then I hung up.

By 8:00 p.m. sharp, I had the signed confirmation from both BMW and Porsche they'd agreed to Wiker's revised offer. I immediately got back on my phone. "Rune, start calling your team. I need everyone back tomorrow." I paused. "Make it afternoon, around 1:00 p.m." It would be a long night at the bar. "I think we've got a solution."

Rune peppered me with questions. "What's happened? What did you do?"

"I'll explain later. Make sure the metal team looks after the system and get on the phone. I don't want to lose anyone."

I was in a rush. It was already past 8:00 p.m., and I wanted to see Hilde. I went down the list of my direct reports and repeated my request as quickly as I could.

Word got out. The pub was packed with people, and when I arrived around 9:00 p.m. everyone already knew. The atmosphere felt electric. It ended up being one of the best parties I'd ever been to. I found Hilde in the middle of the crowd with her eyes dazzling, lips tantalizing, and face radiant.

"What did you do? How have you done this?" she said quizzically. Then she grabbed my hands, held me close, and kissed me. A cheer went up from the crowd of onlookers. I felt as if my heart had come back alive.

One of the reporters, Roar Greipsland from a paper called *Fædrelandsvennen*, had followed the team to the pub that night. He wanted to get the inside scoop straight from the factory workers. He was in the thick of the crowd right when the news broke, so he had just enough time to change the paper's headlines: *15:00 factory closes and all lose their job; 21:40 contract is signed. There is new hope...* It all seemed official now.

The festivities were in full swing. Cato Kjorrefjord, the owner of the pub, decided he would create a new cocktail called "The Buhive." I had too many Buhives that night. It was remarkably easy to drink, but it packed a wicked punch— sounds about right.

I remember feeling the happiest I'd been in a long time with Hilde by my side and surrounded by the team—my team. I was happy about something else too: my decision to reschedule next day's meeting to the afternoon. I'm not sure too many people would have made it to work at 8:00 a.m. We all celebrated like we had been spared our lives—because we had.

Despite the previous night's festivities, I was still up early enough to see Farsund at its absolute best: bright and beautiful, with the scent of wildflowers mingling with the salty aroma of seawater. When I arrived at the factory, the parking lot was strangely empty. As expected, no one was at work aside from my management team. We all gathered in Rune's office for our usual early morning chat and cup of coffee. Everyone only had one question on their minds: *What would the automakers do?*

I told them Roth had already been in contact with me. He'd explained they needed paperwork signed and then they could wire money over directly, but it would take a few hours. Sure enough, as soon as the money was wired, Roth sent a letter to Wiker and me saying Porsche would "definitely pay the agreed amount." This time he attached a copy of the transaction stamped and signed by the bank.

Around 10:30 a.m., Wiker arrived from Oslo together with his law firm partner, Erik Sandtrø. They'd flown into Kristiansand, hired a BMW convertible and, because the weather was so nice, they'd taken the roof down. Both wore white slacks, shirts but no ties, blazers, and cool shades. They looked like extras from *Miami Vice*, not bankruptcy lawyers.

"Morning, both. I hope this goes well today. You do know the press will be here, right? You'll have your pictures taken. You'll both look way too cool if things go wrong." I was attempting to lighten the mood, but tension filled my office as Wiker, Sandtrø, and I sat waiting.

Meanwhile, for the second day in a row, Knut idled in the bank's foyer. He was waiting for Johnny Sorensen, the bank's manager, to give him good news. As 12:45 p.m. approached, he'd been there for almost two hours. Tense and bored, Knut called me. Wiker and Sandtrø listened in.

"Boss, I'm still waiting for..." He trailed off. "Wait, Johnny just called me into his office. I'm going to put you on speaker." For a moment the line went quiet, but then I could hear them again. "Can you still hear me?" Knut shouted into his phone.

We could hear everything clearly, even Johnny clicking away at his computer as he checked once again for the factory's bank balance.

"Do you know how much money came into your account?" he asked in astonishment. We could hear Knut muttering, desperately trying to pull the answer from Johnny.

"You just received $13 million! I don't know what you're doing up there, but this is unbelievable."

We'd done it. The factory was back, and so was my dream of making it work. I knew now I could get my Farsund back on its feet, proving how vital these people truly were to the global economy. They were the real assets. Equipment is just a lump of metal, monitors, and buttons. You need people who know how to use the machines.

The next month would be tough, not just for me but for everyone. We were full of uncertainty, as the war was far from over. Yet we had just scored a huge win, and it was time to share the spoils.

Both Wiker and Sandtrø looked as happy as I felt. "Right," I said. "It's time to tell the team." I stood up from my desk, and we walked out of the office toward our team meeting room. The reception was overflowing with reporters, double the number from yesterday. I asked them to wait until Wiker and I had a chance to meet with the factory folk. Although they agreed, an army of cameras followed us as we walked down the long corridor to the canteen.

You could hear a pin drop inside the canteen even though it was crowded wall to wall. Everyone had shaken off their hangovers and made sure to get there on time to hear the latest. I dove right in.

"First things first. The money came in. You're all hired again." The first cheer.

"It's not fair you've had to put up with this uncertain chaos. You should be compensated fairly. So, until this is over, I am going to double your salary, and I'm going to backdate that to the beginning of May." The second, louder cheer came. They never would have imagined this.

"I want every one of you to stay right here. I need you all, now and in the future. You should be rewarded for your loyalty." You could hear a lawn mower in the parking lot next door. Everyone had gone dead silent. They didn't want to miss a thing. "So, I will pay each of you $16,000 as a retention bonus if you stay with me until this gets concluded, which will be no later than July 28," exactly six months after the first day of bankruptcy. A half-hearted cheer followed. *Did I say it wrong?* Turns out no one knew what a retention bonus was.

Wiker translated what I'd said into Norwegian without the word "retention," and then everyone started clapping and roaring with approval.

Nothing can fully describe the whirl of feelings in the canteen that day. Yesterday they had all been sacked, and now they had double pay and a bonus to look forward to. It was Thursday afternoon on a brilliant spring day, and Monday was a national holiday. I told them to go home, enjoy the long weekend, and celebrate.

Then we let the press in. They were greeted with euphoria, laughter, and tears. Cameras flooded the room, but we just didn't care. Wiker and I bathed in the moment, mingling with the joyful crowd. Jan Ove, in disbelief, looked me straight in the face and said, "You've just put millions of dollars into the local economy—in the middle of a global recession."

Kristin Ommundsen came up and hugged me. She had tears of joy in her eyes. This was her hope, her way of protecting her children and her life. As I left the canteen, we both walked into the Workers Union office. They had fired up the waffle griddle, and the delicious aroma wafted out into the hall. The press followed us with their cameras to capture our broad smiles for the front pages.

Meanwhile, darkness descended on the offices in Germany. Solbach and Roth had shown me how they thought, what they feared, and how they acted. I had promised Karsten they would pay millions. It did indeed cost them many millions. And it was going to cost them many millions more.

CHAPTER 17

Cast-Iron Contracts

——

JUNE TO JULY 3, 2009

As I turned around, Hilde stood proudly in white panties on a huge granite rock, framed by ferns and delicate lichen. Minutes before she had been fully dressed. Her golden hair caught in the slightest puff of a warm breeze. Her eyes matched the deep blue of the sea far below us, and like each ripple, they sparkled in the sunshine. I have never wanted anyone so much as I wanted her right then. On the side of that mountain that day, drenched in the early summer sun, we made love, real love.

Afterward we sat naked on the warm rock, overlooking the majestic fjords. Hilde lay between my legs, her back against me as I wrapped my arms around her. We soaked in the moment.

This was my new reality. I had all the motivation I needed to make Farsund my new life.

What happened in the last week of May had been a real victory, but that was in the past. After a meeting in Oslo with all parties—BMW, Porsche, Alcoa, and the government agencies—I'd been going crazy trying to figure out a long-term plan. Now, on the first Tuesday in June, Hilde insisted we go for a mid-morning walk in the mountains. Her passion helped me think clearly.

"So what is it actually going to take to fix this? For good, I mean."

I thought for a moment, my mind wandering away from the beauty around me. "That's a very good question. I need new orders to fill up the factory. It will take years."

"What about BMW? Can't they just give us back everything they took away?" I could tell this was what she'd assumed would happen.

"I'll try, but I don't trust them. Once they have control again, they'll crush us. We are on the radar of every executive at BMW and Porsche. I'm the buccaneer." I squeezed her close. "That's what I have to be. Farsund has to be the victim of a pirate."

She thought for a moment. "Then you're free to do whatever you want." She continued, "BMW doesn't need us for too long, but Porsche needs us." She knew exactly what I was thinking.

"Yes, yes they do. I'm going to get them to sign long-term contracts where they give us all the cash we need to keep the factory up and running." My plan sounded ludicrous as I said it out loud, but it was all I could think of.

"You'd better make those contracts unbreakable. Use Porsche to keep BMW there." Of course, a Mexican standoff—Roth could help me write the contracts. Porsche could be the police too.

The wheels in my head were spinning fast. "I'll have to act crazy and panic them into this. Give them horrible alternatives that make this their best option. I'll be a true pirate."

Suddenly a chill wind interrupted my train of thought. It was time to get dressed and get back to work.

"June's going to be fun!" Hilde said sarcastically as she put her bra back on.

Soon enough, factories around the BMW empire started to run low on our parts. They still hadn't paid their bills, so we hadn't shipped them anything for over two weeks. Their fleet of empty trucks remained parked around Farsund, idling.

Eventually the pressure became too great. BMW cracked. By June 8, every invoice was paid. We instantly restored the supply chain. Castings started to flow off the production line and into those empty trucks. The drivers were all delighted to stop camping out. As beautiful as Farsund was, they wanted to get home. Well, almost all the drivers. Those collecting parts for Ferrari were a little sad. They'd ventured into town during their enforced stay, met some local ladies, and enjoyed their time.

Of course, I wasn't the only one hatching a plan. I was summoned to BMW's inner sanctum, the FIZ, once again. This time, they made sure I traveled with a lawyer representing Alcoa just in case I let anything slip during our trip. Information would give them leverage. This time, they invited me to the glitzy high-end meeting suites. This time, I didn't need to go through the lengthy security protocols. I didn't get tossed into an endless succession of gloomy corridors. I didn't get assigned to a basement room full of broken furniture. Instead, I was taken to a large room lined with windows, fully functioning furniture, and framed portraits of the latest BMW creations.

Everyone had already packed the room, waiting for me. Roth looked menacing, as usual. Dr. Schleinitz looked confident, even jovial. It was his time to shine. He had filled every seat with thirteen other lawyers, some from Porsche and others from BMW. Most importantly, he had brought along his superior, the esteemed Philip-Christian Eller, one of the senior members of the BMW management board who had signed the fake payment documents back in May. I was deliberately positioned at the end of the U-shaped configuration of tables—the accused on display.

Schleinitz's objective was to get a hold of the agreements I had to buy the assets. Those critical documents were all stuffed into a red folder lying on my lap. On the front of the folder, I had written the words "World Domination"—a joke to myself. None of those documents had been signed by the bank; none had been executed—exactly what he wanted. His team of lawyers were ready. I tried to stay calm.

Schleinitz stopped chatting with his boss and stared directly at me. In the patronizing tone of a true BMW lackey, he said, "Mr. Cockroft, we have decided to save your company. You don't need to worry anymore. We want to ensure *the long-term continuation of your company*." I had heard this last phrase tossed about endlessly before by both Roth and Solbach. But their words never matched their actions.

"We're on your side," Schleinitz assured. No one from his legal team looked up as he spoke. They kept their heads buried in the files in front of them, as if making eye contact with me would break their poker faces.

Finally he got to what he wanted. "We may even be interested in buying the equipment from you. So we do need to see the contracts that prove you own them. Can you share those with us, please?" He threw the bait on the table. I'd been cast as a greedy crook, intent only on getting rich.

I scanned the room. All eyes now focused on me, alert to my response. "We are not here to discuss assets. I am here to make the business work again. I need a busy factory. I need orders." At first I felt completely vulnerable for saying this, but my logic made sense. Clinging tightly to the red folder, I stuck to my agenda. "What new orders are you going to give the factory?"

"But, Mr. Cockroft, we're here to help. Don't you see? We have decided to save the company," he said patronizingly.

But there were no new orders. "Can you or anyone else around this table tell me what new orders you can give me?"

"Yes, yes," he replied hastily. "We can discuss all that later, but right now I do need to see those contracts." He held his hand out toward me. I took a quick glance at the red folder again and tightened my grip. I didn't budge, and the meeting fizzled out.

I woke up in a sweat at 2:00 a.m. My mind churned as I stared at the ceiling and thought about that meeting. I didn't stand a chance of winning. I would end up a fool, a joke. Worse, they would make sure everyone knew this. They would publicly execute me, so no one ever thought of repeating what I had done.

Then I thought more. I'd been in this same situation before when I fought for my father's business. I'd learned to use every single resource I could get my hands on. I'd learned to look hard into my opponent's world because it gave me an understanding of how they thought. I still had enough to fight—and more.

I witnessed something in that meeting in Munich, confirming what I'd sensed for months: how the cogs of BMW actually worked. I remained a mystery to them, but meanwhile, Schleinitz had unwittingly exposed their inner workings to me. The way Solbach operated wasn't exceptional. Solbach reflected the culture of BMW. Everyone in his world respected BMW's convoluted hierarchy because it would crush them if they didn't. But they'd become too complacent wielding that type of power.

I refused to play by those rules. I could be agile. I could make decisions fast. They were too big for that. BMW's chain of command had to be navigated. It took them too long to act. They were brutal but slow. I could use their sloth to tame their strength. I could antagonize them by making wild threats. I could direct their own arrogance against them, so they'd become their own worst enemies. In pursuing their self-interest, they would instinctively chase me down a path, one I had actually chosen; a path that would trap them.

I jumped out of bed and grabbed a pen to jot down my thoughts. I would need to scare them, lead them to the brink of destruction. And I would blame all of my actions on the meeting—Dr. Schleinitz in particular.

Finally, I fell into a deep sleep. The next morning I would unleash the mayhem of a mad man.

The morning of June 10, I sent a formal response to Schleinitz's meeting—a terrible offer I knew they couldn't accept. I revealed I'd created another company, Buhive LLC, a shell company in the US which now had an exclusive license for all the assets in Norway. It made ownership complicated and it meant they had to follow US laws. It confused their lawyers and made it more difficult for them to outsmart me legally.

Next, they had just twelve days to pay me millions of dollars for July's production. Then the price would more than double for every month after that.

Then it got dark. I introduced the prospect that one party may run away from the deal. Should that happen, then the other party would have to pay the missing piece. This was aimed at getting Porsche's attention.

Then I offered them an option to buy me out for $60 million.

I finished my offer with an ultimatum: "If none of the above options are acceptable then the assets will be mothballed for six months, and no production will take place while restructuring is underway." I hoped the final punch added fear.

Just to prove my intent, I copied Degler into an email chain, as though it were by mistake. The email she received was my reply to a quote from a company I'd asked to disassemble, pack up, and store every last machine in the factory. They had to believe I was preparing to execute my threats.

It worked. I got their attention, and they panicked for a couple of days. It was exactly the distraction I needed to quietly close the asset purchase agreement with Landsbanki. Alan McClaren finally signed them over to me. The contracts Schleinitz was so eager to see were now fully executed.

My scheme did make the management board of both Porsche and BMW scramble. They had no other option but to negotiate with me for something more reasonable. Something, days earlier, they would have never accepted.

On Thursday, June 18, I went to the Radisson Hotel at Oslo Airport to meet with Roth, Degler, and Solbach's boss, Joachim Goldbach. All three had been tasked by their superiors to put an end to the mess they faced. The time had come for me to get what I really wanted—a real long-term solution to keep the factory alive, but under my terms.

Roth called me before the meeting started. He had a message to deliver from his ultimate boss, but it was a secret message only I could hear. He told me to keep this morning meeting between ourselves—meaning Goldbach and BMW must not know.

We sat tucked away in the corner of the hotel lounge area. Four blue, felt-covered seats surrounded a low coffee table. Roth and Degler had come straight from their plane. Roth looked furtive, constantly checking the entrance and darting his eyes from side to side. He then said conspiratorially, "I want you to know I've been authorized by Dr. Wiedeking to give you whatever you ask for. I will be tough on you in front of BMW. Goldbach is going to be really tough. But don't leave. Hang around after the meeting, and we'll get this done."

Then they both stood up and walked to the elevators. I hadn't seen Roth like this before. He wasn't angry. He treated me as if I were part of his team, allied against BMW. And strangely, he seemed genuine.

I gave them ten minutes before I headed to the triangular-shaped meeting room. Roth and Degler acted nonchalantly when I entered, continuing to talk to Goldbach. Goldbach didn't greet me and looked furious. I ignored him and prepared for my monologue.

What I said next would be the foundation of Farsund's existence. It would govern how we would live our lives. I had to be clear, powerful, and confident. I couldn't show any doubt or fear. I thought of Wiker. *I need to be Wiker today.*

I moved the flipchart into the center of the room. Then I proceeded to write down the terms I was willing to accept. When I finished writing, I looked at the other three. All had gathered around the flipchart. They were captivated—but not in a good way.

"This is a long-term solution. Success means I have to win new customers and new business. So, all agreements will be for five years." I then picked up the marker and slammed it against the first bullet point. "We will launch a new company. Farsund Aluminum Casting, FAC. It will take over any business the bankrupt old company had."

I moved down to the next bullet point. Their eyes followed the pen. "We will jointly own this company. We will all be able to see what the others are doing." This was the start of my Mexican standoff plan. Porsche had to be able to keep tabs on what BMW was doing. It was the only way I could turn them into the contact police.

"I will run the company and expect to be paid in the same amounts as has been normal for my services. Initially, you both will give me enough cash to operate the company." They knew that would be millions. "You'll give it to me as a gift." *Ouch.*

Next I discussed all the orders BMW and Porsche would keep with us for the following five years. They would not be allowed to move any of them, even if they made a new version of the same car. We'd get that order too.

Then I got to the part of the deal that would be the hardest to swallow. "I will try and run the company profitably, but it won't be until I get new orders. Therefore, you will agree to pay me anything I ask from you. I don't care if we are screaming at each other. It will be paid within six working days of my request."

I'd demanded an open checkbook. I'd made them think I was crazy, that I was prepared to close the factory down. June was coming to an end. Everyone was running out of time. They had no other options.

"I will own the assets and lease them to FAC. It will cost $2.2 million a year to rent." I just picked a number at random. I expected they'd push back hard on this, but they didn't.

I let my words sink in. All three picked through the bullet points, one by one, muttering in German. Obviously, the bullet attracting the most interest was the open checkbook. BMW would pay the lion share of all my requests, much cheaper for Porsche than Roth had anticipated.

"Do you agree to these terms?" I spoke with a cold, deep voice, trying my best to copy Wiker's tone. I needed them to remember Wiker would hold to deadlines. I needed to remind them Wiker was still there, in the background. Adopting his manner also boosted my confidence.

Roth talked to Goldbach in German for a few minutes before finally saying, "We agree."

"Good, then sign the flipchart paper, please." They both grudgingly signed it, and then I signed and dated it.

"You have three days to get me your letter of intent. That's Monday, June 22. After that there is no deal. On Monday all employees will be given their notice again. All operations of the bankrupt estate will terminate on June 30. Either the factory closes, or the new company will take over from that point. You have your work to do. I won't detain you any longer." I thoroughly enjoyed the Wiker approach. Like donning a mask, I could hide my doubts, my fears, and myself. I wished this persona were really mine.

As he gathered his papers and put on his coat, Goldbach looked at me incensed and hissed, "You are utterly despicable, Mr. Cockroft!" Was that it? Not as bad as Roth had predicted.

With the meeting over, I jumped on the silver express train heading to the center of Oslo. It whisked me out of the airport through stunning fields, forests, and fjords until it dropped me in the heart of the city. The royal palace loomed directly ahead of me as I walked up the street to Wiker's offices. It was time to fill him in.

A call came in from Roth on the deadline Monday, June 22. He didn't seem angry. He was just desperate. "I am not able to get a letter of intent to you today, Mr. Cockroft. There has to be a change. BMW and Porsche cannot both own a company. Our legal team say it's a conflict of interest and we would need special permission from the European courts."

I looked out of my office window. This was a problem I hadn't thought of. But Roth was eager to tell me he'd already solved it. "Therefore, I propose Porsche will take BMW's share. I have it all written, but I need to get both senior management of BMW and Porsche to agree to the letter."

He had been working hard, but I wouldn't budge. "I don't trust you, Mr. Roth. Work harder. Call me back by 5:00 p.m. or I will shut the factory down again."

At 5:00 p.m. he phoned again, begging for one more day. I adopted my Wiker tone again. "The bankrupt estate closes in a week. We are in the same place we were less than a month ago. You know how this ends. This is your very last chance."

"I promise this time we are doing it your way." He did sound sincere. He also sounded exhausted. To prove his point, he sent a letter stating Porsche and BMW would pay all invoices after June 30, including the electricity bill. It was signed by Roth, his boss Harter (Porsche's financial chief), Goldbach, and Eller (BMW's head of supply chain).

The letter of intent finally arrived via fax on Tuesday, June 23. It was exactly as I'd spelled out in Oslo—no corrections, signed by the same four as yesterday's letter. I called Roth again. His assistant put me through straight away.

"I have done exactly everything you have asked for, Mr. Cockroft. You have no reason to change anything," Roth insisted.

"I don't think it's me you need to worry about. I'm here. I'm committed to this, Martin. You should worry about BMW. In my experience they always agree to one thing then do something completely different. Let's face facts. They only need us for six more months. Then they can just go away; drop us. Think what that would do to you. How much would that cost you?"

I had him cornered and needed to make sure he knew it. "These contracts we're writing up to match the letter of intent—I'd make them bulletproof, Martin. Unbreakable. No, it's not me you need to worry about. I'm not going anywhere."

Roth remained silent, pondering my words. He had to manage both BMW and me.

On July 3, 2009, all contracts were signed and executed. Money was transferred into the accounts of the new company, Farsund Aluminium Casting. A long-term future had been secured by contracts that were so bulletproof, so unbreakable, and so generous; an open checkbook for the next five years— free money.

CHAPTER 18

Rock Star

JULY 3 TO 23, 2009

"It's payout time." I roared with delight. "Who wants their bonus?" I joked with the team. The payment of 100,000 Kroner, equal to just over $16,000, was on its way. "We'll pay that out on Monday."

I looked at Helge, my HR director, for confirmation. He nodded in approval.

"Your jobs are back for good too." Pause. "If you want to work here." I wore a huge grin on my face as I delivered the news. "Thank you for staying with the factory and believing in me."

Pandemonium erupted across the room—roars, laughter, applause. *We'd done it.* That day, Friday, July 3, we got our future back. The craziness had ended, and we intended to celebrate.

What did this mean for the team?

Rune Svestol bought a super sleek, red and white Ducati motorbike and a matching leather riding suit, the first of many superbikes in his life.

Cor Pronk bought a collection of woodworking tools he'd been dreaming of. He went on to make home furniture and toys for his family, repair boats for his friends, and build many other things. He still has them to this day.

Kristin Ommundsen finally could pay off some of her debt. Without that burden, she could fully enjoy her life in Farsund, surrounded by her kids.

Geir Falkum and his wife Eleanor felt secure enough to start the next generation of their family. Six pounds and eleven ounces of joy blessed them several months later. Many others in the town followed suit.

Winning meant different things to different people. Generally, though, Farsund was on the up. We had faced a bleak future, embroiled in a nasty fight with the odds stacked against us. Now we could finally revel in our unlikely victory. My reward was their happiness. They trusted me more than I trusted myself.

Yet we all shared the same lingering thought: *Is this new "real" real?*

The contracts were bulletproof, policed by Porsche. Millions of dollars sat in the bank. We had just enough business from BMW and Porsche to keep everyone busy. The new company had been launched: Farsund Aluminium Casting

A.S. Everything appeared stable... as long as I never stopped fighting.

There's no such thing as a win-win. Someone always loses. You just have to choose whom you fight for.

Meanwhile, in Zuffenhausen, Stuttgart, no one quite knew who they were fighting for. The month of July brought sheer turmoil. The aspirations Dr. Wendelin Wiedeking had of attaining 75 percent of VW evaporated. The lauded leader of Porsche—who wrestled the company out of financial disaster in 1993 when it was worth only $300 million and grew it into a formidable industry titan valued at $25 billion, recognized as the European business leader of the year by *Fortune* magazine, and the architect of the most audacious commercial hijack ever seen in the automotive industry—stood at the edge of catastrophe.

He picked a fight with the wrong man at the wrong time: VW chairman Ferdinand Piëch. Piëch was the grandson of none other than Ferdinand Porsche, the founder of both VW and Porsche. He sat on Porsche's supervisory board, and his family controlled just under half of the board's votes. No way would Piëch let an outsider take control of the family business. And he would not hesitate to use brute force to prevent that from happening.

Wiedeking's scheme fell apart financially too. The Great Recession left Porsche short on cash, and borrowing money became expensive. Wiedeking borrowed ten billion euros to buy every last VW share he could to attain the magically controlling 75 percent he needed—considerable debt, especially for such a risky move. In that market, because of Wiedeking's recklessness, Porsche faced the same financial instability that had plagued them in the early '90s. Piëch used raw fear of failure to harness the support of the Porsche family. He then publicly denounced Wiedeking, discrediting him for spending so much money.

On July 10, 2009, just one week after Farsund's contracts had been executed, Wolfgang Porsche, the company's chairman, called for an extraordinary supervisory board meeting. Wiedeking had been summoned to attend—one last chance to revive his plan and salvage his career. But Piëch still had no intention of letting this upstart win. The board meeting would be used as a slaughterhouse.

Less than two weeks later, Wiedeking incited rapturous applause as he addressed more than five thousand workers in the heart of Porsche's Stuttgart headquarters. It was perhaps his most inspiring speech. But then, it was also the eve of his execution. He delivered one final message: "We should not look back, no matter what happens. We should now work constructively on our future."

According to the Associated Press, Wendelin Wiedeking and Holger Härter "came to the conclusion" Porsche would be "better off" without them. They both saw the step as necessary to calm tensions between the two firms and clear the way for a merger. Porsche would now become a subsidiary of VW. Piëch and his family had assumed ultimate control and limitless power.

The removal of Wiedeking and Härter changed Martin Roth's world. He had faithfully followed Wiedeking's instructions to mitigate the risk that the Farsund factory had imposed. He had been commended for writing the cast-iron contracts, those robust and unbreakable clauses that kept the factory open and BMW in check. But in the blink of an eye, his mentors were suddenly gone, and Roth became the author of an embarrassingly generous mistake. I think at this moment he began to hate me.

CHAPTER 19

Bubble Pop

——

JULY 28 TO AUGUST 31, 2009

I saw the newly designed HQ only from the outside. I imagined Porsche's management board room in Stuttgart looked modern, grand, powerful, and intimidating. Three feet above the floor rose a podium, upon which sat a dozen silver-paneled desks, connected and arranged in an arc. The arc focused on one thing: a plain table at floor level. This was the interrogation table, lit by spotlights to stand out from the darkened surroundings.

Up on the podium, Wiedeking had once commanded from the center desk. Now that spot belonged to Michael Macht. As one of his first tasks, Macht had summoned Roth to this room to appear before the new management board. Roth's torture would begin here, at the interrogation table, where he would have to explain those contracts he had authored.

The board repeatedly asked Roth one question: *How on earth do you give someone an open checkbook?* That's exactly what he'd done. I called it the "cash call," the telephone conference we'd have every other month when I demanded the cash I needed. They would have just six days to pay. Roth would have to present my demand to this management board and then face a shower of queries and criticism until he received their approval. He would have to coordinate with his BMW counterparts. And finally, he would have to actually send the money as requested. His actions were bound by the contracts he had to uphold.

I could feel the tension, and I used it. I used him to police the system. He would have to chase the money down and make sure I was paid on time. Tension came at a price. Roth remained supremely dedicated to Porsche, his community. I infuriated him every time I insisted on more money. And I kept making him focus this fury on me because it was the only way I could divert his attention from Farsund.

It felt like dancing in front of a tiger, dressed like a deer. Sooner or later, he'd pounce.

No one in Farsund cared about the details of this corporate intrigue. All they believed was they had a sorcerer on their side who made magic happen. Less than one week after Wiedeking's deposition, the Farsund Avis headline on July 28 proclaimed, "Veni, Vidi, Vici." I was famous. I was rich. I was invincible. I was loved.

Summer in Farsund felt like paradise. I was perched atop the A-list now, with my face in every newspaper and constantly on the TV. People wanted to hear me speak at clubs and gatherings. They invited me to every party in town. They wanted to help me and spoil me. A pint was bought for me in any bar. I was offered a rental home exclusively on the island of Farøy, a luxurious four-bedroom abode facing the sea. It was owned by the Glastad family, one of the richest in the region. This wasn't on the market or rented out, but it was made available to me.

I could have anything. I already had everything. A beautiful girl, my own factory, a new home, a new car (courtesy of Porsche), and several bank accounts stuffed full of cash. This was my new life. The pink champagne kept flowing, and I was carried away in their river.

Norwegian labor laws have a vacation rule. Between the end of June and the end of August everyone is entitled to three weeks of vacation. These weeks have to be consecutive, and they are paid for by the company. FAC closed in the last week of July. I went back to the US.

The taxi dropped me off at the bottom of the driveway next to the three-door garage. It was evening, and night was settling in. Cicadas chirped in the woods surrounding the house. I was home again after a day of flights. I tapped in the code that would lift the middle door and watched as it opened. Everything seemed normal: three cars parked in their normal spots; my tools exactly where they should be.

I opened the final door from the garage into the house and was greeted by three kids and two dogs, each desperate for my undivided attention. "Daddy!" they all shouted. The dogs couldn't wag their tails fast enough, pushing the kids away and grabbing all the affection they could get. They knew nothing about my new life. They had no idea their own lives would soon change. They just loved me.

Fuck! What am I doing? In Norway I was the super-warrior, the King of Farsund. In America I was something else, but I wasn't totally sure what. I remembered I was a dad. *How have I forgotten this? What sort of animal am I?*

Charlotte greeted me politely. "All your furniture has arrived," she said. I'd ordered a whole house load of furniture to ship to Norway. It was much cheaper that way. I would take my Porsche too.

"It's a little crowded at the moment. When are they picking it all up?" she asked as I followed her to the front of the house. We'd bought a big house, but we couldn't even get past my new furniture to the front door.

"Wow, look at all this stuff," I said in amazement.

Charlotte echoed me. "Yes, look at all this stuff." She had sadness and bewilderment in her eyes and her voice. We thought we had accepted the reality of our separate lives, but perhaps it was harder than we wanted to admit. "I miss us," she said and then steadied herself. "I've put you in the guest room. I hope that's all right. Or we can swap if you want my bedroom."

It used to be our bedroom, but not anymore. I was her guest now. I knew things about this home only our family would, such as how the screen door to the back deck squeaked and where every plate, pot, and pan lived. But it wasn't mine.

I'd created another reality in another country, one that had ruined my marriage. My children didn't know where I lived or what my new home looked like. They didn't know anything about who their father had become. I suddenly realized I had carelessly shut them out. I had been so focused on saving Farsund. I hadn't thought about them. The very reason I'd traveled to Farsund two years earlier was to provide for and protect my family. I was still paying the bills, but was I protecting their emotions? Was I being their dad anymore? I felt sick to my stomach.

At that moment, I knew my world had changed. I had to put together the remains of my fragile family first, even though I could not fix what I had already done to them. Whatever I created in Farsund had to be a home for them too. They were number one. Not Hilde and her children. I would have to live alone and wait, hope, for my children to join me. I knew they couldn't and wouldn't move to Norway, but I had to leave the doors open for them anyway. No one else was allowed in. I had no idea of how to build a new life that wouldn't wrack me with guilt. I'd created my own hell.

Over the Atlantic, on the plane heading back to Norway, I put all my feelings, emotions, and hopes for a normal life with my family in a cast-iron trunk, impenetrable as a fortress. I locked it tight and then pushed it deep into the bottom of my soul. I had plenty of those trunks down there. I'd collected them since childhood.

Deal with what's directly ahead of you. Focus on work. Here at least, it was clear what I needed to do. The new company, FAC, had to start from scratch. I had to build our business, win new orders, and convince our skeptical supply base that we—that I—could be trusted again. Most of all, I had to contain and control my sponsors within Porsche and BMW.

Like Roth, I'd created my own hell. Like Roth, I hated me too.

CHAPTER 20

Porsche Regret

——

SEPTEMBER 2009

We were dropped off in front of the iconic gates of Ferrari's original headquarters and factory. Two pillars, with the prancing horse logo emblazoned on each, supported the gates. It was late summer of 2009, and I was in Maranello, Italy, to attend a meeting with Ferrari's design engineering team, along with Jan Ove, my technical director. We were trying to convince them to choose us for more business.

Our host arrived quickly to give us a magical tour. First, we went to a hall stuffed full of Scuderia racing models, the hand-built conclusion of the F430. Each car received personal attention from a dedicated team. Talk about a kid in a candy store. I wanted one. Then we walked through an entrance in the factory wall to the next section, the new F458 production line. It was like stepping into a time machine and arriving in Tomorrowland. That Ferrari had become one of the world's leading manufacturers was clearly evident.

After the auto-orgasmic experience, our host took us to the design team offices on the factory roof, a modern glass atrium structure. Overlooking rooftop gardens, the offices seemed spacious and tasteful with glass panels separating the working areas. Jan Ove and I were seated in a room in the center of the structure. Our host asked for our patience and left the room.

Through the glass walls we saw him walk over to his boss, who turned, looked at us, and grabbed his phone for a short conversation. Then they both walked back into the room. He introduced himself as the manager of the supply chain department. Suddenly there was a knock at the door. This was the director of the department; then another knock, now the vice president for engineering; another knock, the vice president for the purchasing group. Successively more senior executives began flowing into the room.

Then Luca Vezzani entered. We'd talked on the phone before when he was in Munich. He'd heard me drop the bomb back in May. He was the one who pushed away from the table and left BMW and Porsche to figure out their problem. He wanted to see what I looked like. Within five minutes fifteen people were crowded into the room and many more were looking in, pressed up against the glass walls. They were thrilled to meet me, but that was all. No new business came—too much risk.

It wasn't just Ferrari. Everyone wanted to meet the infamous Mr. Cockroft who had defeated BMW—"the biggest buccaneer on this planet," as Lutz Johanntokrax, one of the most senior engineers in Mercedes development team, called me. Meeting me gave them status with their peers.

But choosing the Farsund factory as a supplier was a different issue. No one wanted to suffer the same embarrassing fate as BMW. No one would be crazy enough to give me new orders. Ironically, my reputation had become the biggest hurdle to Farsund's survival. The only way I could break out of this trap was to focus on technical expertise. I could use facts to quell fear.

In many industries, especially automotive, the choice of who supplies parts isn't actually made by the purchasing department. If you're at the forefront of technology, the design engineering departments choose. Engineers pick you if you can design unique parts quicker, solve their problems better, and get testing done faster. It's too late for the commercial departments to make a decision by the time you've created a part meeting all the technical geeks' desires. You've become a unique supplier, and your part is already locked into their new car's design. All the purchasing experts like Solbach can do is to argue about the price.

So I focused on honing our technical capabilities. I built an amazing team of experts and engaged with our customers' geeks.

Yet something was still holding them back, like a dark force that couldn't be seen. It locked them into unification. It was calculated. It was consistent. And it was everywhere.

A clue spilled out when a technical team from Audi visited Norway. They were one of our biggest target customers. If we could convince them of our value, our prize would be a contract to supply parts for their latest car, the Audi A6. That car was made in such volume we'd be profitable even if we only made one part for every third car. I was ready to put on our finest show.

I welcomed the team the night they arrived together with Karsten Mohr, who'd traveled with them from Germany. After dinner concluded, our guests retired to their hotel rooms. We had planned a full schedule for the next three days.

Karsten stayed back. He had a message to deliver. "They were told not to come. They didn't know exactly where that order came from. They just knew it was from someone high up their management ladder." He had his usual grin and a look of intrigue in his eyes.

"So why'd they come? Why waste a whole week?" What I was really asking was why they had disobeyed command.

"You. They want to see if you're really the asshole they've been told you are."

His answer kept me awake all night. I sat on my balcony. The sky was crystal clear, dotted with a million diamonds. The moon's reflection on the sea illuminated the granite coastline. The view should have calmed me, but my mind was churning. Every customer I chased had the exact same story and even used the same words. *Don't trust Cockroft. You'll regret it.*

How were they all so coordinated? Then I remembered the secret meeting the German automakers had every week where they discussed supplier issues and agreed how to handle problems. I'd learned of it at the start of Farsund's bankruptcy. Every week I was asked for so much information from Porsche and BMW, right up until 11:00 a.m. on Thursday. Then I'd get the same feedback from them and from other customers too. I thought it was a coincidence at first but it happened again and again. It was one of the few places where coordinated decisions were made, decisions that could ensure orders flowed or were cut off. This was Solbach's domain, a place where he could dispel any doubt I was anything but a treacherous pirate.

I'd been hearing plenty of rumors running through the industry. One claimed I worked only 50 percent of the time and flew first-class to Florida every month for a two-week vacation, courtesy of Porsche. I thought about this quite often as I racked up my usual fourteen-hour day, seven days a week. I couldn't be sure if it was Solbach, but someone was setting the scene for what was to come. The days BMW needed us were gone. Only the contracts kept them tied to us. BMW would want to find a way out, and Solbach would want his revenge. I thought, *He'll do something. I don't know what. But it's coming.*

The following weeks were full of demands from Solbach's and Roth's teams. They both asked the same questions at different times and in different ways. They wanted to know how many parts we could make if we worked twenty-four-seven. They wanted to know how much space we had to store the parts we made. They even asked if we could rent somewhere to store more parts. They made all sorts of claims as to why they needed this information even though the reason was obvious. It appeared as if they were dancing around each other, but I sensed them working on a shared plot.

Things became clear after a difficult board meeting for the new company, FAC. At the meeting, Roth appointed a lawyer who acted as the chair. Roth went crazy when I pointed out he was breaking the company protocols. Then he demanded I should simply comply with his will. He told me I would have to pay any legal fees. It was his way of rubbing in his authority. His instructions were heard by everyone in the room, including the lawyer's assistant, Anna.

As instructed, Anna sent me an invoice one week later. The invoice contained clues I wasn't meant to see. I opened the envelope and noted the quality of the paper: expensive, watermarked, heavy gauge. The invoice detailed a slew of activities and meetings, hours spent by a team of lawyers who had all flown to Munich. It even called out the attendees at each meeting. Roth was there, and so was Solbach. It was clearly an active project. It even had a title: Project Storm.

BMW were finding a way to break my Mexican standoff. They went to VW directly, the new owners of Porsche. The VW executives didn't like the Farsund situation. They wanted it to end. They couldn't believe only Farsund could make that one precious part. The executives at BMW, Dr. Herbert Diess in particular, had opened up discussions with VW's leadership. The objective was to move on. Restore control and finish the Farsund fiasco. Project Storm was being managed by Solbach.

CHAPTER 21

The Spiral

———

OCTOBER TO DECEMBER 2009

"What about this one?" Stein Age asked, using his chin to draw our attention to his find. Stein ran my IT department and wasn't used to scouring the seashore. Well, neither was I, Frank, or Rune. All four of us were dressed in our factory workwear—blue trousers, matching jackets hemmed with high-viz reflective tape, and bright red hard hats—casually wandering down the beach.

We had come to this beach in Borhaug to find a rock, but not just any rock. I wanted the perfect rock, a symbol that would last for eternity. It would live at the reception entrance to the factory. I planned to have a small brass plaque engraved and fitted to this rock. It would represent the local region: granite-hard and resilient but rounded and smoothed over time by the sea. Also, it was cheap. But since we didn't want anyone to see us steal it from the beach, we were trying exceptionally hard to blend into the surroundings and not draw attention to ourselves.

We strolled along trying to look innocent and gazing out at sea with our hands in our pockets. Occasionally one of us would nod at a rock, and then we'd all shoot stares at the specimen and debate under our breaths about its particular merits.

Finally, Rune found the perfect one. All four of us gathered around. Two acted as lookouts while Rune and I tried to pick it up.

"One, two, three… go!" I said.

We learned a lot that morning. We learned quickly granite rocks are deceptively heavy. All four of us couldn't lift it at all, and what was worse, we had aroused the curiosity of one of the locals who started to walk toward us. We had about two hundred yards to get another stone before he was upon us. We dropped the pretense of innocence then. What the hell, we were rock thieves and proud of it. Rune shouted he had the ideal, though much smaller, candidate.

Like a well-oiled, four-man machine, each grunting heavily, we lugged the new rock to the car. Each of us shouted out opposing instructions. Finally, we landed the beast in the trunk of my car. We were proud of ourselves—until we noticed how close the oncoming army of spectators had gotten to us.

"Quick. In the car!" I shouted. We took off.

"That's Tor Javid. He does our transport," said Frank. *Bloody small communities.*

On October 7, exactly a year after all the chaos had started, we celebrated the official launch of Farsund Aluminium Casting A.S. We put the rock on display in the canteen. It had a brass plaque that read, "July 2009—A new start," along with the Buhive logo, now FAC's. The logo contained a hidden reminder. It represented my three children who underlay everything I did. Now I could see my logo every day: on letterheads, in presentations, on everyone's new uniforms, and lifted high on the flag outside the factory.

As fall arrived, my new life fell into place. The new house was complete, and my furniture from the States arrived and fit in nicely. I had a new company car and my private Porsche I'd imported from the US with the furniture. I was adopted by a group of friends, all about my age. They joined me in the sailing club, the scuba diving club… practically any club I wanted to be part of. I could have any material thing I wanted.

What I couldn't have was what I wanted most of all. I couldn't have my family. I couldn't have Hilde either. We both tried so hard. Hilde looked on as I set up my new home. We went shopping for household goods, vacuum cleaners, fridges, and washing machines. She'd point out the ones she'd choose, so I'd buy two of them and give her one. I knew it was not what she wanted.

I figured if we went away from the town, a weekend in Oslo, Kristiansand, or Stavanger, we could escape to a sort of bubble and create our own reality. I'd revert back to spoiling Hilde all weekend. It became my way of apologizing. We'd make love, again and again and again. Then we'd fall asleep in each other's arms.

But every night my three children would join me in my dreams. I would hear Victoria ask me, "Why, Daddy? What did we do? Why have you abandoned us?" as she held her brothers close. She'd be wearing a pink, ankle-length night dress, and the boys would be in their pajamas. All would gaze at me with the most desperate looks on their faces, as if straining to understand why I deserted them. I would wake up at 3:00 a.m. awash with guilt.

A cycle was born. I would isolate myself until I needed company, and then Hilde would always welcome me. We'd head out of town again and go to wild, no-holds-barred parties. But once the fun ended, the guilt and self-hatred would return. I'd push Hilde away, isolate myself, and lock out any chance of happiness. I'd get creative when it came to punishment. I would run for miles and miles until I felt exhausted and ready to collapse. Then I'd eat crap, like raw cabbage and ketchup, for a week.

For Hilde's birthday, December 7, I wanted to do something for her, something I'd never done before. So I planned a getaway trip to London. When we arrived at Kristiansand airport, we didn't need to go through security. We were above normal protocol. An impeccably dressed German pilot was already waiting to greet us, the VIPs. "Please follow me, sir," he said as he escorted us to a minivan that ushered us through the security gates onto the tarmac. There, we saw a private jet, its doors wide open, beckoning us inside.

As soon as we took off, the copilot offered us champagne to toast the start of the most extravagant weekend I could have imagined—filled with Broadway shows, Michelin-starred meals, and executive suites in Mayfair five-star hotels. I showered Hilde with fine jewelry, clothes, bags, and shoes—anything she wanted. In return she gave me her body, wrapped in the most sheer and lacy lingerie. I could and did everything I wanted with her. It felt like a rockstar's life.

But when the weekend ended, I knew things had spiraled out of control. We arrived back in Kristiansand, and she left to join her family for a Christmas gathering. As I drove home alone, I had the same gut-wrenching feeling of being trapped in paradise. My community respected me as their hero. Hilde loved me. But I'd rejected her, and I'd abandoned my children and my family. I'd broken every promise I'd made to always put them first.

For the first time in my life, I spent Christmas alone. I ate cold baked beans directly from a can and then got drunk and passed out.

CHAPTER 22

Small Thinking

JANUARY 4, 2010

Project Storm was ready. Frank Solbach had woven a vast web. This web stretched into every department throughout BMW. He controlled where multiple millions of dollars were spent every year. He could make businesses succeed or fail. He could make managers throughout BMW superstars or incompetents. He had the power to solve production problems, quality problems, and design problems. Problems came and problems went, poof, at his whim.

He pulled all this off by managing upward. He didn't want to be in the spotlight. He didn't want his name attached to any decision. He preferred to exert his influence from behind the scenes. He used his own boss, Joachim Goldbach, as his weapon. Supported with carefully edited "facts" and rumors, Goldbach became one of his most effective tools. Through him, Solbach could feed the message and the direction he wanted leaders to follow.

Toward the end of 2009, rumors started to circulate throughout BMW. *We were poor at running the factory. We made bad quality decisions. Our engineering skills were weak and very limited. Ultimately, we were greedy, worthless swindlers who didn't care about our customers.* None of that was true, of course. We had an amazingly talented team, deep industry experts in all fields, with a loyal commitment to our customers.

The rumors painted a dire picture, but not enough for BMW to break its commitment to Porsche or its new goliath parent, VW. Still, Solbach wanted out. He wanted to win. He had already duped Porsche into Project Storm. He had already started to build up enough parts to make it easy for BMW to change suppliers. He even convinced Roth the factory could be sold to manufacturing giant Georg Fischer, while in reality he was hunting for something else.

That "something else" was the one clause that killed all the contracts: an "unquestionable and unsolvable quality problem." A problem that made some parts wholly unfit to use and unable to fix. This was something BMW couldn't ignore and couldn't live with; something that would empower the leaders of BMW—the board of directors, in particular Dr. Diess—to abandon FAC and, with it, Porsche.

Although our factory was up and running, for me things were quiet the morning of January 4, 2010, the first working day of the new year. The bright mid-winter scenery was calling for me to enjoy it. Farsund barely has six hours of daylight during the winter, but today we had been rewarded with such beauty. The sky was cloudless, and the sun was vibrant.

The mountaintops were capped with bluish-white snow, accentuated by dark gray crevices. More snow lay deep and crisp across the buried fields.

I'd spent the weekend learning to ski cross-country, Nordic style. It felt wonderful to get outside, fill my lungs with fresh air, and exercise. I mingled with families and friends taking ski routes through the woods. Occasionally they'd stop, light a small fire, find a log to perch on, gather round, and drink hot chocolate from a thermos flask. It didn't matter how cold it was outside. Extra layers were always available to throw on. The Norwegians like to say, "There's no such thing as bad weather, just bad clothes." I was an awful skier and spent the weekend falling. Luckily, I had good clothes.

Today was another perfect day to ski—what I wouldn't have done to be out there. Last week I'd finished all the year-end reports, so now I had a rare lapse in my workload. Our customers' corporate teams, including Solbach and Roth, along with most of their production plants, were all on vacation. My phone was silent. Production was running smoothly. We had enough money in the bank. I had nothing to do. So I walked into Hilde's office. I wanted to persuade her to sneak out and come skiing with me.

"I'm bored." I sighed and slumped into her spare chair. "I'm not very good at being bored." She knew. "Got any coffee?"

Distracted from her computer screen, she swiveled her chair to face me. I pointed to the flask on her desk. She looked beautiful in her signature black leather jacket and stylish blue jeans. It was her eyes that captivated me, though. They sparkled like bright gems, lighting the entire room. Hilde smiled as she reached for the flask.

Suddenly the smile dropped from her face as she looked at the door. Knut Pettersen, head of the quality department, rushed in. He'd come straight from the factory. Pettersen rarely looked flustered, but right now he seemed desperate and scared.

"We've got a problem," he exclaimed. "I had a report from BMW saying they had rejected two parts just before Christmas."

My mind was racing. "Have we got them back yet? Can we see what's wrong?"

"No, they said they needed more time to inspect the parts." Pettersen seemed impatient. This wasn't the point.

Then I said, "When were they made?" Alarms were going off inside my head. Was this another BMW gambit?

"Both were made in the bankruptcy period." There was more to come. I could tell from his expression.

Hilde piped in. "That's before the contracts came into effect." She knew exactly what I was thinking.

"So not FAC then. We had so much disruption in that period. One or two parts with surface defects could have slipped out." I sighed. This couldn't break our contracts. The parts were made during the time of bankruptcy before FAC existed. It meant they couldn't use the quality clause. The bad news was coming.

Pettersen continued, stumbling over his words as he tried to translate from Norwegian what he actually wanted to convey. "That's the background. The real problem has just happened."

He stuttered over the next words. "Another part actually cracked in a car. It made the rear suspension collapse."

I was too shocked to respond.

Pettersen continued, "The car was already delivered to a customer in China. It sounds like the owner wants to sue BMW." It just kept getting worse. I closed my eyes and scrunched my face. The big question: *Was it made by FAC?*

"It's definitely one of ours. We made it in August."

There, the final blow.

Pettersen blurted out, "You need to call Henrique. *Now!*" He was shouting by this point in sheer terror.

Henrique Adao, director of new projects for the factory, answered immediately. Alois Rankl, head of the quality department at BMW's Dingolfing plant, had already called him with the news. "The Dingolfing team are scrambling. Alarms are going off everywhere." I could hear his deep apprehension over the phone. "I need a cigarette."

Henrique took a drag from the cigarette and exhaled loudly. "Rankl has put us onto the quality council meeting agenda."

Dr. Rankl reported to a cross-functional team of experts, chaired by the corporate quality head. This quality council managed problems all the way to the top—the board of directors. Thus, control the council and you'll control the outcome. Solbach knew this very well.

Knut Pettersen's eyes widened and he cradled his head in one hand. This was the third part that had broken in just one month. All of them were for the new model five and seven series cars. He couldn't believe it. He'd been with the plant since it was launched. He was employee number six, head of the casting process. His team defined every step needed to make a *good* part. In all that time, we'd produced parts for more than four million cars, and he had never seen anything like this.

I certainly wasn't bored anymore. We now faced a crisis. It was bigger than my issues, bigger than the factory, and bigger than Farsund too. Real people, drivers and passengers of BMW's cars, could be in danger. Parts could fail, cars could crash, people could get hurt or, worse, die. We needed to find out what was wrong—and fast.

"Get Reza, Per Erik, Kristen, and Jan Ove." I ran off the list of world-class experts I needed for what would surely be a team effort: two PhDs, all four with master degrees in engineering from some of the world's best universities.

Then I looked at Hilde. "Get Rune, Frank, and Cor Pronk." This was the key operations team dealing with production and quality.

"We meet in the production meeting room in ten minutes."

I told Rune to stop production and isolate all parts. We couldn't let anything out of the factory. Then I turned the machines over to the engineers. They would need unlimited access to any equipment we had so they could run loads of experiments.

I had only a week to solve this problem. Now wasn't the time to fight with Solbach. Now was the time to figure out four things: what caused this failure, how many bad parts were out there, how to detect a bad part, and ultimately how to stop this from ever happening again. My team got to work.

Over in Munich, Solbach had been gifted with the perfect scenario. At the very least, he could use this mishap to further ruin FAC's reputation. And if he tried really hard, he could build it into an "unquestionable and unsolvable quality problem," thus invalidating our contracts.

But the BMW network was on winter vacation. Their offices were empty, their lights were off, their emails went unread. People wouldn't return to work for another week.

Solbach had trapped a fly in his web, the very fly he had been eyeing all along. He just didn't know it yet. The clock was ticking.

CHAPTER 23

A Sting in the Tail

___

JANUARY 5 TO 12, 2010

Casting machines are mammoth: three stories high and buried ten feet into the ground. They are constantly fed by a dedicated robot arm that stuffs the molds with sand cores and then waits to whisk away parts once they're cast. The parts are placed onto an enormous conveyor system that sweeps up into the rafters, eighty feet above the ground, and on to the next step in the production process. Seventeen of these giant, sophisticated machines fill the three-hundred-thousand-square-foot factory. They emit a constant cacophony—the sound of industrial progress.

But today, January 5, 2010, the factory was eerily quiet—aside from the occasional sound of Kristin shouting instructions to her colleague, Per Erik. Both were fully focused on discovering just what had caused BMW's parts to fail.

"Cycle number 214. Oxides go in both left fill tubes." She reached over the open machine and stuffed little shavings of oxides into the tool.

Once out of the way she said, "Okay to cast." On her command, Per Erik cycled the machine as she observed her next experiment, one of eight hundred they'd carry out.

The casting process started. Molten aluminum was pushed and sucked into the huge and highly complex mold. It then flowed into the cavity in a precise way, specifically designed by engineers and repeated every time a cast part was made. But somehow a problem had emerged. BMW had found some castings had broken. The part was made weak by a shriveled up film of oxides. It could break when it had been assembled into a car. Worse still, it couldn't be seen before it broke. We had to work out what caused it and how to stop it.

Kristen Ommundsen and Per Erik spent the next seven days doing nothing but trials and experiments. They cast thousands of parts and tried to reproduce the failure BMW had found. They systematically changed every parameter to get a complete picture: temperature, fill time, time between each cycle. They got a bunch of oxides and stuffed them into the fill tubes. They even cast parts contaminated with grains of sand. Every parameter was recorded and correlated.

We then X-rayed and destructively tested each casting, pulling it apart and seeing where it broke. It will always break at its weakest point. We examined the parts under microscopes to try to pinpoint the cause. It was always an oxide. Then we chemically analyzed what we found. It wasn't from the crucible. It wasn't sand. It wasn't a ceramic chip from the fill tube itself. It was aluminum oxides from the side wall of the tubes that pulled the metal into the mold.

Meanwhile, Dr. Reza Babaei had started a series of simulation tests. Remember, we had state-of-the-art simulation software. We could simulate casting a part in just two hours. That means we could make a mathematical model to track every single molecule of metal as it enters the mold, with every parameter, in every microsecond. From start to finish, from hot to cold, we could change parameters, even adding simulated oxides. We did over thirty different scenarios. To do one simulation at BMW took between seventy-two and ninety-six hours. It was the same with all our competitors. We were world leaders in this field.

What he found amazed us. Reza simulated oxides and added them to the model. Because of the part's design, these oxides got caught in the flow, in a kind of vortex, and eventually landed at the exact spot where we saw failures. Kristin and Per Erik copied the simulation for their real-life trials. They got the same result.

Other designs didn't have this bottleneck flaw. That's why we'd never seen this before. This design, the BMW design, made the part have a bottleneck. Metal couldn't flow easily into the cavity. The bottleneck trapped these nasty oxides. Getting oxides in a casting will happen, but it's normally okay because they end up in areas where you can clearly see them. This design was causing a problem.

Now that we identified the issue, we had to solve the issue, but first we had to be able to spot bad parts before they went to BMW. It meant changing our inspection process.

People always get caught up with inspection. *If you know what you're looking for, you can find it.* That's sort of true, but you can't inspect quality into a part. There will always be some mistakes people miss, no matter how observant they are. We had to have an inspection protocol, and I didn't want to trust human intervention alone.

We went for an automated solution, something that would pick up this oxide problem 100 percent of the time. To do this we called our X-ray software experts and started to work with them on a solution: a 3D filter that let a computer see right through the part from all angles. This was completely new.

Finally, how do we stop this from happening in the first place? First, we looked at changing the casting procedure. What if we brushed the tube between every casting cycle; coat the fill tube with a special lubricant; throw out the first two cast parts after stopping casting for more than fifteen minutes? All of those had no effect. Some actually made things worse.

We could change the design of the part. We simulated new designs until the bottleneck flow went away. It was doable, but not really practical for BMW. New parts would cause all sorts of problems for them: new tools, more testing, expensive and long.

"We have to find a way of living with this bottleneck," Kristin concluded. Per Erik, Jan Ove, Reza, and I were back in the production meeting room as Kristin explained the alternatives. It was late Thursday, and we had just three more days before Solbach and his team would pounce on this opportunity.

"How about trapping the oxide before it gets into the part?" I thought out loud. "Put a filter at the top of the fill tube?" I was far from being the expert in the room. I was sure this idea would have a flaw. But everyone stopped and turned their attention to my proposal.

"We could use stainless steel filters. They won't melt. They can take much higher temperatures than we ever use," Per Erik chimed in. He looked upward as he visualized the process. "But they would have to be replaced every time a part was cast."

"We can add them to the gripper arm," said Kristen, referring to the robot arm that picked up the castings between every cycle. "Then the robot can fit them into the mold."

Trials started the next morning. By Sunday we'd run another batch of two hundred parts. We shoved oxides into the fill tubes and then added a filter to the top of the tube: 100 percent captured, 100 percent success. Every part tested good.

Per Erik and I walked out of the factory back to the office. "Is this definitely systemic? Are you 100 percent sure?" I asked him.

"Well, there is always a degree of uncertainty," he stated in his usual "consider all the options" manner. "But in this circumstance, yes, I'm certain this is the design of the part."

For a moment I contemplated Solbach. *He has no idea what is about to happen.*

"Keep dedicated to this problem. I want the whole team to collect irrefutable evidence of what the problem is and, importantly, how to fix this. I want that X-ray solution finished too. How quickly can you do all that?"

Per Erik's eyes stared up to the left. You could see him mentally walking through every step needed to complete my request. Then he looked down to the floor and said calmly, "We should be able to get this done in six weeks."

"I'll need an interim report at least, before the end of next week. It has to have your best estimate of how many cars could be out there running around with bad parts. Possible?"

"Uh, Yes…" He drew out his answer. "We can get that done."

"Good. We'll be going to Dingolfing to present it to Rankl before the quality council meeting. They need to focus on the problem." I finished and walked back to my office.

Solbach hasn't caught a fly in his web. It's a big nasty wasp with a brutal sting.

PART 3

SOLIDIFICATION

CHAPTER 24

Recall

Do you know how many parts go into making a single car? Around thirty thousand.[1] *Some are simple nuts, bolts, or washers while others are incredibly complex. Some parts are absolutely critical to the safety of the vehicle and, most importantly, its occupants. Some parts use the latest cutting-edge technology in their design, functionality, or capabilities. There are many different categories, but one common theme is every single part depends upon all the parts surrounding it.*

Each of those thirty thousand parts has its own engineering drawing.[2,3] *The drawing specifies every last detail: material, dimensions, mechanical properties, color, durability, even strength. Each part also has a prescribed manufacturing process, testing process, and inspection process the vendor must follow before the parts can be delivered.*[4,5]

The parts we made were "safety critical." Safety critical parts can be in all sorts of places: tires, steering controls, fuel systems, engines, electrical, or structural components. Like links in a chain, it just takes one to break and the whole system fails. The car is then unstable, potentially out of control, and life-threatening. You can see why these types of parts demand the most attention.

That's the critical point. It's the responsibility of everyone involved in making those parts to ensure they are good: the designers, the people who make the parts, and those who assemble them. If they don't do their best, lives are at risk. It's a moral responsibility the whole industry must embrace.

Carmakers have an army of experts to police the manufacturing and assembly process. Their quality organizations essentially act as the guardians. They check the designs. They define the tests and inspections step by step. Everything is examined and recorded, from certificates proving raw material conforms to tightly controlled criteria, to which parts were delivered to the carmaker and when. Every part has its own unique path that must be traced by data. [6,7]

Why is everything so tightly controlled? It's the only way automakers can be completely sure everything has been done right; that the parts are going to be safe. Follow all the steps, do them correctly, and nothing bad should happen.

Mistakes do happen. If a safety critical part starts to fail, those experts need to know why. They need to know what caused it to fail, when the problem started, why, and how many parts are bad. They need to find them all; trace them all the way through their system and into the cars that used them.

Sometimes they can't. Either they can't find the problem or they can't fix it. That's when things get very messy and very expensive. Blamestorming starts. Who caused this problem? The automakers will blame the vendor, and vice versa. Decisions that caused this critical problem are exposed. Sometimes it's because of design, sometimes it's because of manufacturing, but more often than not, it's because of penny pinching. The true moral nature of these companies is exposed.

In 2001, Firestone, the automotive tire manufacturing giant, and Ford Motor Company became embroiled in a controversy regarding an unusually high number of accidents in the Ford Explorer and other similar vehicles. What caused these accidents? The tread of the tires essentially came off while driving.[8,9]

They tried to bury the problem for years. Ford and Firestone knew they had an issue five years before the recall. They just didn't categorize it as significant. They knew fixing it would be very expensive. Maybe it would simply disappear. They wanted to keep bad news away from the press and away from government officials.[10,11]

This debacle resulted in 271 deaths and eight hundred injuries.[12] The actual number of fatalities may have been much higher, but Ford and Firestone found a way to blame some fatal accidents on other issues.[13,14]

Once the problem went public, the finger pointing began. Firestone blamed Ford for the implementation of a new type of suspension, which had been shown to cause cars to flip over in high speed pre-production trials. Ford could have reengineered the suspension, but instead they opted for a cheaper solution. They lowered the tire pressure of the front two tires. It worked but came at another price. It also decreased the durability and life expectancy of Firestone's tires.[15,16]

Ford took Firestone to court, claiming the failures were caused by shoddy workmanship and inappropriate materials used during the tire manufacturing process. Ultimately, both parties were ordered to fix the problem and keep their customers (and the general public) safe. Only one solution existed: to replace every single tire on 1.3 million vehicles—a recall. The federal stipulation is that you've got to have a huge pile of good parts to replace the bad ones before you start a recall, at least 40 percent. So they needed 2.6 million tires before they could start the recall. The only way automakers can make that many spare parts is to close down car production and divert the supply of tires to the recall efforts. They couldn't make a single car until the recall started. The result: a huge loss of production and a huge loss of sales.[17,18]

In 2001, Ford actually went further and replaced the tires of another 2.6 million vehicles. Imagine that: just under twenty million tires changed out in dealerships, tire shops, and certified maintenance facilities; a logistical nightmare at exorbitant cost. Firestone claimed this effort cost them $2 billion. Ford said their bill amounted to $5.5 billion. On top of these whopping costs are endless other issues: lawsuits, loss of production, loss of sales, and loss of credibility in the market.[19,20]

In reality, any recall is extremely damaging, especially for the one that takes the blame. The automaker will always try to blame the supplier along with anyone else outside of their company. As everyone dodges accountability, the moral equation gets flipped. Individual safety seems to take a back *seat to money, power, and status. It becomes a real mess. It's certainly news no automaker wants.*

Even a little fly can deliver that news if they have enough hard facts.

CHAPTER 25

Rabbit Hole

———

JANUARY 14, 2010

"You're really going to rent that?" Per Erik smiled for the first time that day. Alongside him, Reza's own huge smile lifted his round face. His eyes radiated disbelief as he exhaled and simply sighed and said, "Yesss," while nodding.

We had arrived at Munich International Airport on our way to BMW's Dingolfing plant to meet Dr. Rankl. This was going to be a tough day, an automotive manufacturer's nightmare. They definitely wouldn't want to hear my message. Regardless, I had to explain what we'd found and why we were certain it was the root cause of the failed parts.

There had to be some good memory Reza and Per Erik could take home from this trip. Here it was. Outside the Sixt car rental booth, a poster stand lauded the luxury of the new Porsche Panamera, enticing customers to rent one. Both my guys had worked exceptionally hard designing the part we made for that car. Now it was time for them to drive one.

They'd only be able to do 125 miles per hour because we had winter tires on, more than double the fifty mile per hour speed limit enforced in Farsund. The bounce in their step lightened our mood on the way to the parking lot.

Per Erik gripped the steering wheel firmly as we entered the Autobahn. "Maybe you should hold on," he said casually as the car accelerated. In the back, Reza giggled and yelled, "Wheee!"

The meeting was not going to be pretty. Two more cars had seen failures: one in Germany, the other in the United States. That totaled four cars since the start of the year. The only good news seemed to be a driver could still control the vehicle when the part failed, lowering the risk of an accident.

I doubt Solbach cared. In fact, the news of these failed parts was probably his version of a New Year's gift.

At an earlier meeting, Solbach's stooge, Goldbach, had demanded the minutes of the meeting "reflect the failed parts BMW's customers have experienced due to *poor quality.*" Roth knew what this meant. He knew BMW wanted proof a quality problem existed. It could ignite Project Storm.

Dingolfing sits alongside the A92 autobahn, showcasing huge lines of factory buildings—one after another, all gray with soaring roof lines. The plant didn't just produce one model here. It manufactured three and four series models and the five and seven in large numbers. It formed the heart of BMW's empire.

After parking in the visitor parking spot, we entered the clean, tidy, and efficient facility. Not one piece of art could be seen. Everything appeared purely practical: white walls, black chairs, off-white desks. The quality department's meeting room looked the same—a collection of tables arranged in a U-shape, surrounding a presentation screen and whiteboard.

Dr. Rankl, a large heavy-set man wearing an avocado-green shirt, was already waiting for us with five of his associates. He sat in the middle of his team, flanked by experts—a mix of design engineers and metallurgists who all understood the casting process. One member of Solbach's team was also present: Harald Hoschek. Hoschek was there from corporate. He worked for Solbach. He would observe and report back.

Standing in the center of the room, I turned to face Dr. Rankl. Reza and Per Erik pulled out our presentation. We were ready to go.

"Thank you for taking time to meet us. You won't like what we've discovered," I said in a grave tone, loudly enough to grab the attention of the entire room.

Rankl retorted, "This is a very serious matter, Mr. Cockroft. I just hope you have brought me encouraging news."

"Well, we've taken all the containment actions you've specified. We found no bad parts." I paused as they took in this news. "But I fear this is false confidence.

"You see, in the past two weeks we have run more than eight hundred trials and a bunch of simulations." Disbelief swept across the room. Rankl's technical team found it hard to fathom such work could be completed in so little time.

"I assume you will give us evidence of this?" Rankl asked, stone-faced.

I nodded. "We've got it all here. My experts will take you through all our findings in detail."

Now I had to drop the devastating news. "What it shows us is this is not an operator error. It's not because of a bad cleaning process. It's not because of any delays between casting cycles. It's not a single batch issue either. This is a systemic problem."

The room fell silent. No one moved.

"It could have happened at any time during our production." Rankl choked on a cough but waved me to continue.

"It's caused because of a design flaw." One of the technical engineers looked to the ceiling in despair.

"We are working on a number of solutions, but based on our trial data, we have estimated there are about 120 parts that are likely to break… already built into cars. They are undetectable." My words found their mark.

"You need to see and understand our evidence before your quality council meeting tomorrow. I think the consequences of this are significant. This is a safety critical part," I concluded. I held Rankl's eyes. A bead of sweat ran down the side of my face.

All automakers have a system that tracks what parts went into what car. If they have a problem part, they can narrow it down to a group of cars that could have had a bad part, but if you can't see the bad part which was made at random, it could be anywhere. All the cars they made could have a bad part.

In this case that included every new model five and seven series which had been made since the start of production back in September of last year—about forty thousand vehicles. I also told them we had no way of finding a bad part until it actually failed, and probably 120 vehicles had this problem. To be sure they captured this three in one thousand fraction of bad parts, they would have to replace our part in all forty thousand vehicles.

I knew Rankl, a blue-blooded BMW man, would push back when he heard this grim news. His team would look at every detail, alert to any potential flaws in our data. But Rankl was also genuine and honorable, believing in doing the best for the customer, no matter the cost. He followed facts, not politics.

"Now, Dr. Reza Babaei." I pointed to the presentation screen displaying our introduction PowerPoint. "Can you start with your simulations? I want you to explain details of the mathematical model you used to simulate the castings. Show them where the bottleneck flow problem is, why it catches oxides, and how the design could be changed to avoid this problem."

I turned back to look at Rankl while Reza prepared himself. "Please ask all the questions you have. I want you to be in no doubt." I then took my seat and let Reza talk.

For the next forty minutes Reza guided us through his simulations, slide by slide. He showed how the vortex formed. He showed how it trapped the nasty oxides in the critical area. He even showed how a design change could solve the issue. Each member of the audience carried doubtful expressions. But as Reza continued, those looks of confusion finally began to shift.

All changed except Hoschek. He continued to appear skeptical.

Next, Per Erik took the stage. "Everything Reza highlighted here has been shown in our physical tests too." He pulled out hard facts, a variety of samples, and laid them on the table. Each had a specific number and a unique data set, covering all the casting parameters, testing criteria, chemical analysis… everything. Now the technical team was fully engaged. They jumped out of their seats and gathered around the samples, examining the oxides, visible at the fracture point, and then comparing the samples with each other and the data on the charts.

After all that, Rankl's team couldn't do much to dispute our root cause seemed probable. But they remained reluctant to fully endorse us. They said they wanted to do further analysis of our data and model the process using the BMW simulator. That would take another two or three weeks to complete.

Next I turned to the crucial topic of solutions. Hoschek, and through him Solbach, had to hear what I was about to say. *We had solutions.*

"We are in the early stages of resolving this problem, but we've run a number of trials and think two solutions will resolve this issue without redesigning the part itself." The BMW designer sighed in relief.

Per Erik then explained the filter that prevented this issue from happening. "The oxides you can see in these broken samples aren't coming from the crucible. We deliberately added them in the fill tube."

He next pointed to clean, unbroken samples—our tangible solution. "But these parts had the same type of oxides added in the fill tube, with the addition of a new steel filter at the top of the tube… And here's the filter encased in aluminum after the cast part. We've cut it in half. You can see the oxide, trapped by the filter, outside of the part. We tracked every oxide for over two hundred trials. Each one was caught by this filter."

Everyone watched intently as Per Erik unpacked ten samples onto the table, cut vertically in half and polished. The oxides were clearly trapped by the filter. They'd been circled with a purple felt pen to make it easier to see. Rankl and every member of his team took a sample and examined it. Intense conversations spilled out as Rankl's team absorbed what they were seeing.

Per Erik then projected a picture of the new X-ray protocol that would catch any parts after they'd been cast. On the left were two X-ray pictures of a bad part. The pictures had been taken exactly from the position Rankl's team insisted upon—part of the quality inspection protocol. You couldn't see the oxide at all. It was completely invisible.

The right of the screen showed several X-ray pictures from different positions. In these images, you could easily see a white shadow buried deep in the part. It had even been picked out by the automatic detection system.

In a calm and knowledgeable tone, Per Erik continued, "We are still working with Xylon on this new system. It's called the Yama filter." Xylon is one of the industry's best-known, nondestructive testing solution providers. The fact we were working with them gave us credibility. "Our plan is to have this fully tested and ready to implement by the end of March."

"You cannot change any inspection protocols without Mr. Rankl's approval," Hoschek immediately chimed in. He'd stayed quiet up until this point.

Rankl looked curiously back at Hoschek and replied, "We will take this into consideration. We will visit you over the next two weeks and review your protocols. I expect you will conclude your investigations and solutions by the end of March at the latest." This wasn't a suggestion. This was a command.

We'd completed what we set out to do: communicate the facts clearly, thoroughly, and impartially. Now we could only wait and hope Rankl and his team would uphold the same standards.

It was Reza's turn to drive as we jumped onto the Autobahn back to Munich Airport. He started cautiously, but things changed once he got the feel of the car. Trucks and cars flew past in a blur. The row of trees along the road melted into one continuous smudge. Racing past at 125 miles per hour, we couldn't focus on any single one of them.

"Why was Hoschek so vocal about inspections?" Per Erik asked, trying to distract himself from Reza's driving. "He looked desperate. Didn't he?"

"He's got to report back to Mr. Solbach. That won't be fun." I stared out the side window across a snow-covered field. Brown stubs poked up through the white sheet: remains from the autumn harvest. I fell into deep thought.

I had wanted to work with BMW from the very first day I started in the automotive industry. In that world, they appeared to be the best of the best. Their tight-knit network felt impossible to get into. If you somehow did, you were anointed as special, supreme, and trusted. It transformed your career and your entire identity. I looked up to them as the pinnacle of style and precision. Fresh out of school, I wondered if I'd ever be good enough to perform in the BMW organization.

That disappointed me the most. I knew them now. They didn't think or act the way I'd always imagined. They were little more than bullies who protected their borders with brute force and intimidation. And now I'd become their enemy, even though I was actually trying to protect them.

The faulty parts vastly changed the positions of our chess game. BMW didn't seem to fully know their disadvantage lay in those unbreakable contracts that dictated what they could and couldn't do to us. An unsolvable quality issue was the one clause that discharged them from their commitments. But I put that clause in for a reason. I knew it could never be used.

"An unsolvable quality issue." Think about what that means. *We have made bad parts, which they had used, and we couldn't find a way of making good parts.* In other words, BMW would have to publicly confess bad parts were in cars they had already made. I'd make sure this went to the press. Redesigns, recalls, customer lawsuits, production stoppages, loss of sales—all these would be possible and even probable if they executed this clause.

I interrupted my train of thought. "Did you see the look on those faces today?" I asked Reza and Per Erik. "Rankl's team were there to call us out. If we'd tried to make this a small issue, tried to hide it, if we'd presented some crap story, without facts, they would have ripped us apart. We were very clear. We backed up everything we said with facts and data—very credible indeed."

I steadied my voice as the pieces came together in my mind. "We told them this is a big problem; something they can't ignore. It's on record. They will have to tell their quality council about this. But it gets more complicated. It means the design of the part is bad. BMW caused this problem. It's their fault, not ours."

A look of wonder formed on Per Erik's face. He now understood. I continued, "Our Italian competitor will have the same issue. It's the same part, and they copied our process step-by-step."

"So they'll have to do something about this?" Per Erik asked.

"Exactly."

The mood changed as the car entered the parking lot of the rental office. All three of us felt a mixture of renewed hope and determination. I looked Per Erik and Reza directly into their eyes and told them what we needed to do next.

"Focus on fixing the problem. Let them discover the rabbit hole they've got themselves into."

CHAPTER 26

Death of a Storm

JANUARY 15 TO JUNE 2, 2010

Deep inside the FIZ, Karsten Mohr scuttled from one room to the next down the endless corridors. Ostensibly he was there to meet with some of the technical teams and talk about mundane, year-end reports required by BMW's various departments. In actuality, he was there for something much more important—gathering intel. Through casual meetings and informal chats with the quality council, he could essentially act as our spy.

The quality council meeting had adjourned two hours ago. Karsten had been productive during the interim. Trying to be inconspicuous, he looked furtively left and then right down the corridor before shooting into a vacant meeting room. He hid himself in the corner and shielded his cell phone as he relayed what he had gleaned.

"Boss, I've had a very informative day. Rankl presented your report and findings. Apparently, he seemed pretty impressed and gave it some credit. But others didn't. They shot it down."

He inferred I would know who had dismissed our findings. I did.

"They did say they'd send a team to audit us. It sounded like their team would fill a bus," Karsten said, as if to console me.

"What do they think caused the problem?" I asked in desperation. We all had a moral obligation to work together to solve this issue, not manipulate the situation.

He paused. "Well, it's you, actually, boss. They said you didn't care and weren't managing the business well." Was this Solbach's latest move? I felt it was.

"They even brought up the new part. Solbach's team really did a good job putting doubt into the council members' minds. Now they're questioning if FAC is good enough to make parts for the M5."

Karsten was talking about the new M5 car, a super-powered stallion that made muscle cars look weak. We'd won a small piece of business to supply a similar part for this car, and we were in the prototype phase. Using the M series' reputation against us, as a weapon, was quite clever. Supplying parts to their flagship car, parts that could break, would certainly rile the souls of everyone in that room, uniting and stirring them into action.

Project Storm sparked to life behind closed doors. Teams from BMW and Porsche met with lawyers from Oslo as they planned how they would use this "unsolvable quality issue" to exit those binding contracts, retrieve some credibility, and reap their revenge.

∗∗∗

With single-minded dedication, they all brought Project Storm to Farsund on a miserable March morning. Rankl and his team arrived at our factory, prepared with their scripts. Solbach had deputized his presence again: Peter Gaehrken, the senior buyer for purchasing, was there to keep the Rankl contingent in order.

This time, the whole of BMW seemed galvanized. I had just one chance to convince Rankl to see the real problem and take it seriously. But the Munich team was prepared and ready.

In even greater detail, we repeated what we'd already said before. We used facts, evidence, and science. Gradually, I noticed Rankl was starting to believe us. He could tell we weren't the bad guys we'd been portrayed as. He finally began listening.

For the finale, we took him to the casting machines. "I want to show you how we can stop this from happening." I pointed at the open mold. "This is where the gunk comes from." I used a ceramic pointing stick to highlight the fill tubes. "It builds up, and then it flakes off. It goes right past all those traps your engineers designed, straight into the part. But we can stop it. We can put a mesh filter in every tube before every part is cast."

I nodded to the machine operator, and he pressed the big black button. Instantly a special robot arm with four fingers swung into action, placing the round mesh filters exactly in position. Then the mold closed. Moments later we had a cast part. The filter acted as a trap and caught any impurities. The part was pure. Rankl seemed convinced. But it wasn't like that for Solbach's disciple, Gaehrken.

"It's not that!" Gaehrken ranted desperately. "It's this stupid fool." Now he was shouting at the casting operator and pointing wildly.

Rankl stepped in. "Calm, Peter. Calm." He held him and looked him in the eyes. "I think we should return to the meeting room."

As Rankl escorted Gaehrken out of the factory, they insisted they needed time alone. I watched them huddle around Gaehrken's cell phone as I left. Another hour passed before they summoned me to return.

Rankl looked like a defeated man while Gaehrken had returned to his usual smug self. With victorious defiance in his voice he said, "We will decide our course of action when we've returned to Munich. Until then you must make no changes, Mr. *Cockroft.*" He emphasized my name with extra hostility. Solbach had the time to manage the situation to achieve the outcomes he wanted. Then people at the top would make irreversible decisions.

Two more parts failed later that month. Then the door shut completely. BMW went dark. We didn't hear of any other failures. We knew they were out there, but someone inside BMW decided not to tell us. It was as if they were afraid to give us too much information and we might use it against them somehow. We were simply instructed to make as many parts as possible.

But I couldn't play this waiting game any longer. I decided to implement the new X-ray software alongside the current system. Technically we were still using the BMW-approved process, but in addition, we were using a process that actually worked. We were now catching that one part a day. The problem hadn't been fixed, but I could check for bad parts before we shipped them. I had a clean supply of parts going to BMW.

As expected, Solbach cancelled the M5 parts order. I couldn't do anything about this. BMW would not have acted without agreement from VW, Porsche's new parent.

***

Once again, Dr. Hubert Diess found himself embroiled in the Farsund affair. Diess held the most senior position in BMW's supply chain and was seated on their management board—a high-profile executive whose outward persona portrayed a consummate professional with extremely high standards and morals. That slick image hid his brutal side. He'd shown me he would use deceit when it suited his needs. Back in May 2009, he had been instrumental in the failed attempt to trick Wiker. He endorsed Solbach's plan and even signed false documents pretending to transfer money to Wiker's bankrupt estate. By doing that, he had lied to the Norwegian government. His tacit punishment was having to live with Farsund. Each time I asked for money, the transaction had to be signed off by Diess. I hadn't gone away.

But now Diess had an opportunity to end this once and for all. Solbach had set the stage, and Diess was ready to pull the trigger.

But Diess had to coordinate with his counterpart before taking any action. He wouldn't concern himself with Porsche. They'd become a subsidiary of Volkswagen. He would only deal with people who equaled his authority—meaning Francisco Javier García Sanz, head of the supply chain at VW. García Sanz worked his way up the VW ladder. He was known for digging deep into issues and rarely missing important details.

He had researched "the Norway thing" from his sources and heard a quite different story. His design engineers preferred to work with us. Farsund was technically competent, was more than capable, and had a state-of-the-art facility. It seemed more logical to fill the factory with new orders and sell it to someone else, someone they trusted—someone in the Mittelstand, a true German-owned family business connected to the automakers' network.

García Sanz's difference of opinion was enough to pique Diess's interest. On the morning of Wednesday, June 2, 2010, he boarded one of BMW's corporate jets bound for Norway. He flew into Kristiansand, where he was met by a chauffeur and a black, long-wheel-based seven series, the top of the range.

As I ushered Diess into the meeting room, Martin Roth and Karin Degler anxiously milled nearby. I exchanged my business card with Diess, and then noticed it listed absolutely no contact details aside from the main BMW switchboard number. He clearly didn't want me to have anything.

We took our seats, and I started with a blunt question. "So, tell me, Dr. Diess, why are you here?" I looked him straight in the eyes.

He was just as direct. In perfect English he replied, "I'm here to see if you're worth saving."

With a wry smile I chuckled. "All righty then. I better show you around."

Normally Roth and Degler wouldn't have joined me during a factory tour, but today there was no doubt they'd be coming along.

We took my standard path tour. First, we hit the maintenance department, then the tool shop. Both were impressive and spotless facilities with clear visual controls. Next, I guided them to the receiving furnaces. I opened the lid to one of the channels that carried molten aluminum from the furnace to the casting machine. We got to feel the heat of the bright orange molten metal. Then we headed to the casting machines. This is where I made a diversion.

"Dr. Diess, I want to show you the part we've had problems with." He walked by my side, his arms held casually behind his back. Roth and Degler trailed behind us. We approached the three BMW-dedicated casting machines.

Reza, Kristen, and Per Erik were waiting for us. Reza had set his laptop up on a stand with a simulation loaded on the screen. Kristen and Per Erik had their own table prepared with props.

"This part failure issue…" I was mindful not to call it a quality problem, as that implicated us. "I don't know what you've heard, but this is my team. All are professional engineers and experts in the field. I'd like you to hear what we found." I felt anxious. *If we get this wrong, we're dead. But I'm telling Diess this is his problem. I'm picking a fight.*

Diess reached forward and shook hands with each of them. Then I asked Kristen to begin. "Can you take Dr. Diess through our findings, please? Don't miss a thing."

For thirty minutes, all three explained and demonstrated the problem, the cause, and the solutions—exactly as we'd done for Dr. Rankl and his team, twice. We showcased our automated robot mesh system, ready to go as soon as we got BMW's permission. But the thing that really captured Diess's attention was our new X-ray system. It clearly showed when a part was bad.

"Why haven't you implemented any of these changes?" Diess asked.

Shocked, I said, "Dr. Diess, we discovered this back in January, week three. We've had the solutions ready to go since week seven. We sent full reports to your team and have been begging to get approval to change our process for almost six months now." I sounded desperate.

"I'm using the X-ray software, so I know we don't send you bad parts. It's the only way I can be sure."

I tried to calm my voice. "This is a design issue. I don't say that because I'm trying to pass blame. Whoever makes this part, using this process, will get the same results. Your other supplier needs to change their process too."

Lunch was waiting for us back in the customer meeting room. Diess sat alongside me, his legs crossed and a plate of sandwiches in front of him. Then he finally spoke. "It seems you are worth saving, Mr. Cockroft. I will call Dr. García Sanz, and we will work on getting you busy again."

By 1:00 p.m., Diess was in his chauffeured car on his way back to Munich. He now knew we had discovered a problem created by BMW's design, and we could credibly explain it if an investigation arose. We could fix it too. We had solutions that worked. He knew all this had been suppressed somewhere in his organization. All this could be made public. It would just take one phone call to the right people from someone with all this information—someone like a disgruntled Englishman.

Before the wheels of Diess's private jet hit the ground in Munich, Project Storm had collapsed. Solbach took a back seat, and soon after he chose retirement.

Now Roth took center stage. Farsund wasn't the bad guy anymore—just me.

CHAPTER 27

Pirate of the Year

JULY 2010

Finally I could be a dad again. For the first time since my
marriage had dissolved, I asked the children to join me for
a month during the summer. Victoria, my daughter, was
traveling in Europe on an extended school trip, so she
couldn't. But my two boys jumped at the chance. Benjamin
was fourteen, and Hugo was twelve. We were going to have
a real boys' adventure.

At last, they got to see where Dad lived; their Norwegian
home. I couldn't have been happier to finally hear their voices
inside those walls. After a short rest, we set off for a trip up
into the mountains. I took them around a lake where a beaver
had made its lodge—a first for them. I then showed them a
field full of longhorn, long-haired cattle—another first. We
laughed and joked as we walked. "What's up with Spud?"
Benjamin asked as Hugo, my youngest, fell over his shoes
for the third time. I figured they must be exhausted, so we
returned home. At last, I could call it home.

I'd been really nervous about their visit because I hadn't had the chance to be a proper dad for such a long time. I worried about details as simple as not being able to cook for them. But now the boys were actually here, I loved having responsibilities outside of my fourteen-hour-a-day work schedule. I cooked up a barbecue with huge steaks, burgers, and fried potatoes. Fortunately, they cleaned their plates. The weather was still warm and sunny, so we sat out on the deck, watching as boats floated by. Later, when it turned cold, I lit the fire pit. I can't remember what we talked about that night, but I do remember more laughs and more jokes. As each boat passed, we'd wave and then shout something—typically rude—at the smiling captain. We did it in such a way no one else could understand what we were saying.

The following day, I took them out on the boat to try and catch some mackerel for our supper. I'm not a very good fisherman, though, and it took some time before we found the right spot. It seemed like a promising area because the people in the boat next to us were catching fish every time they dropped their lines into the water. We spent thirty minutes in the exact same spot… but nothing. Finally, Benjamin got a bite and reeled in his catch. Just as we were about to land, though, the thing jumped off the hook and, with a little wiggle (and what I'm sure was a fish wink and smile), splashed back into the sea. We decided to have pizza.

Monday came, so I took the boys to the factory. I planned to have them work for two weeks and then get two weeks of vacation. I didn't want them to seem spoiled, and I wanted my factory team to see them working hard. I paid them $16 per day for an eight-hour shift. That amounted to $2 per hour. The basic wage in the factory was $25. Since they were too young to labor in the factory itself, they worked outside sorting scrap aluminum parts, painting forklift trucks, and shredding paper in the offices.

During my boys' second week in Farsund, I was planning to have our usual sandwich lunch when Hilde came to my office and announced it was a FAC tradition to have a summer production planning meeting in town at the local restaurant. The boys were invited too. The town was already packed, and a stage had been erected at one end of the square to celebrate the start of the Kaper Festival—two full weeks of fireworks, concerts, and entertainment.

The festival centers around Farsund's history as a pirate town. Farsund and the surrounding community once thrived on this very lucrative but perilous business. Each year at the start of the ceremony, the elders of Farsund choose someone who has demonstrated outstanding achievements that benefit the local community. The kaper, or pirate prize, is inspired by the town's past, paying homage to the bands of pirates who bravely fought off enemy frigates.

I stood in the sun surrounded by my management team and my children. The announcement began. Hilde stood by my side and translated for me. The presenter started to reveal details about this year's winner.

"This year's winner is not from Farsund," the presenter declared, with an air of mystery to his voice. "He knows business. He enjoys being outdoors. He likes to run." Fact after fact was listed, but it was still a mystery. I looked around the packed audience, trying to spot who it could be.

"He came here from America, but he was born in England." I'd gone bright red by now. I realized I'd been set up, and this surprise had been kept very quiet. The organizers pride themselves on keeping the identity of the awardee very secret. I can honestly say I hadn't a clue. To be fair, though, this wasn't difficult, because until that day I didn't know anything about the award itself. Hilde had been in on the whole thing and had even given the prize committee some of my life details.

As hundreds of people looked on and cheered, I walked up to the stage. I thanked the presenter and tried a speech in Norwegian but quickly swapped back to English. The press took pictures of me with my sons, and the local radio station interviewed me. As the mayor greeted me, he grabbed my hand. It reminded me of the last time he'd shaken my hand in the streets, on National Independence Day (May 17) the previous year. So many things had changed since then.

Later in the day, the boys and I rode our bikes through town on the way to the beach. As we passed through, people shouted out congratulations and tried to shake my hand or high five me. I felt so honored to fight for this beautiful community and could not have been more proud my boys were there to share this special day with me.

July rolled on. Benjamin, Spud, and I drifted into a summertime daze. We ran or cycled everywhere as we explored our breathtaking surroundings. Often, we'd bike to the beach and buy ice cream, then just lounge around and chat about anything and nothing. The month flew past, and all too soon, we'd reached the eve of their return to the US. I decided to take the day off work and spend time with them out on the waters. In the evening, we would moor alongside one of the islands and sleep on the boat.

I've never really liked camping. A close encounter with a slug once turned me off to the whole experience, and anyway, there's no room service in a tent. A boat would be different, though, I told myself. Unfortunately, I didn't plan too far ahead for this whole expedition and forgot bedding, toilet paper, and flashlights.

After a day of unsuccessful fishing and general mucking around on the boat, I navigated us to the island of Prestøy. We docked there, then set off up the small hill that marks the inland of the island. I found a picnic table with a view out over the harbor area of Farsund. I did remember to bring a disposable, all-in-one barbecue tray—"easy to light, easy to cook," the packaging claimed. I set it on the table. While it heated up, Spud told me he needed the bathroom. Both Benj and I said he'd have to use the woods, so he set off to find an appropriate tree. A few minutes later we heard him shout from the woods, "Dad, where's the loo roll?" *Oops.*

"Leaves, son. Look for some leaves." What a terrible dad I was. "Oh, my thumb's gone through!" was Spud's next shout. I guess if I'd done just a little more exploration of the island, I'd have spotted the three perfectly well-equipped public restrooms fifty yards from where Spud was now squatting.

Oh well. Hindsight is a wonderful thing, and anyway, I had other problems to deal with. They were right—my barbecue tray had heated up quickly. Now it was incinerating the table I had perched it on. It's very hard to move a burning barbecue.

After we extinguished the barbecue and ate our dinner, we sat around the boat and watched the magical sunset, which, at that time of year, stretched into 11:30 in the evening. The last rays of sun draped the town with a golden aura and glittered along the ripples of the sea. Farsund is a place that takes your entire life to experience. Just when you think you've seen everything, a whole new facet opens up, full of things you would never expect. These islands are a perfect example of exactly what I mean.

I had never seen such broad smiles on both boys' faces. They had loved coming to Farsund, and this marked the start of a family tradition. Over the course of their visits, they met friends who took them out on adventures. They jumped from bridges and let the river carry them downstream. They leapt from diving boards into the sea. They learned about Norwegian culture. The friendships they made then followed them back to their home in America. Visits started back and forth. Suddenly the two worlds of Farsund and Annapolis no longer seemed separate. Farsund had become part of my life. I'd passed it on to my kids, and now they were passing the American experience on to their friends from Farsund.

Unfortunately, low points always follow high points. My boys and I had to say our goodbyes as summer came to an end. I would be on my own again in Farsund. I wouldn't be a dad for another year. What had been our home instantly turned back into just a house. One or two reminders of their visit remained—a discarded sock or a souvenir hastily bought then forgotten. Each one made me feel sick, like I had abandoned them.

Work again became my savior as something I could bury myself in. I felt grateful for the endless distraction. I was still fighting for Farsund. The battle took my time. It took my attention. It took my emotions.

CHAPTER 28

The Wrath of Roth

SEPTEMBER 2010 TO MAY 2011

"Why is it all companies in financial difficulty seem to collect awards, like this piece of shit?" Martin Roth lazed in his office chair as he pointed his pen dismissively at the oversized, aluminum-spiked trophy. Karin Degler, sitting at his side, gleamed back in agreement. I sighed as I stood in front of his desk. I felt like a naughty schoolboy about to be punished. Once again, I was back in Stuttgart at Roth's insistence. This time, we were meeting in a new office, one Roth had borrowed for the day.

The previous evening in Essen, Germany, FAC and the Porsche design team had won the bi-annual European Aluminum Award, the rough equivalent of an Oscar in my world. The award certainly gave us credibility and good publicity—just what we needed to win the confidence of new customers. But Roth said he saw no value in it. To him, nothing regarding Farsund seemed to have value.

He made no attempt to hide his foul mood as we began our conversation. "Porsche has experienced a change in leadership," he announced. He was referring to Michael Macht. The last "pureblood" Porsche CEO had survived for a little more than a year in Wiedeking's shoes before being ousted. Now Matthias Muller controled Porsche. Muller was a true VW guy, which meant Porsche was no more than just a subsidiary of Volkswagen's empire.

"We have decided the best course of action is to sell Farsund Aluminium Casting." Roth kept his expression neutral, but as much as he tried, a slight scowl dashed across his face.

Degler looked pensive, perched on her chair, clutching her files close. "We feel this is the best way of achieving a long-term continuation of operations in Farsund." *There it was again.* I hadn't heard that expression for a while.

"I won't tolerate any of your nonsense this time," Roth said. "If you don't agree with our plan, I will shut you down myself." He couldn't contain his disgust for me. It showed in his expression and in his tone.

Farsund was now VW's problem. Solbach had been removed from the fortress of power he'd spent a lifetime creating. Farsund had a pirate who was seen as the culprit. No one at BMW wanted to be near that issue when Solbach had gone. They also had no need for Norwegian parts any longer, so Diess must have tossed the problem to García Sanz to deal with. It was, after all, VW and Porsche's unique part dilemma. In return for VW's agreement, BMW promised not to relocate their orders. But Porsche's new CEO Muller didn't want to inherit what had become a catastrophic embarrassment either. The problem had arrived back on Roth's desk. He was blamed for creating it and thus tasked with solving it. I was a credible threat to his career, just like I'd been for Solbach. I had become his punishment, which meant I was also his target.

Only two weeks earlier, Roth had been interviewed for an article in a trade journal.[1] He preached the virtues of his impenetrable protection system. In it, he lambasted weak suppliers. He boasted about the risk radar he'd developed that would spot any such weaklings, way before they became a problem. He made it clear Porsche would act quickly and effectively if his radar spotted a problem—actions that would "lead to the termination of the business relationship and a shift in scope."

I'd made him break every single one of the rules he trumpeted in that article. The truth was he was exposing his empire, the one he so proudly defended, to new and significant risks. He was intimately involved in every aspect of a failing supplier. In fact, he was their chairman. Worst of all, he was having to pay vast sums of cash again and again to prop up this hated supplier.

I knew I could use that hate to draw Roth's attention away from the factory. He could blame me for anything bad—if he got me. I hoped he'd be willing to concede to many more requests from whoever bought the factory. He'd find ways to give them new business and fill up their order book. A *true* "long-term continuation of operations."

I was about to paint a big red target on my chest. I steadied myself and looked him straight in the eyes. "Money, Mr. Roth. Money, and lots of it." I could see rage rising in him. "That's the only way I'll let you take this factory from me."

Those were my last words in that meeting room. I achieved my objective, and the process to sell the factory began again.

***

Fast forward two months.

"Um, excuse me." A polite Asian gentleman caught my attention in the reception area. He belonged to a three-person group. "Can you tell Mr. Cockroft that he has visitors, please?" I could guess from his accent he came from China.

He must have noticed my confusion. I didn't have any visitors scheduled for the day. I'd certainly seen many over the last few months. Eight "investors," as I was instructed to call them, had visited Farsund. All were potential buyers, and all were part of the German automotive network. At first they were escorted by Roth, but he soon lost interest. It seemed he'd lost any care.

After a tour, we got down to the details. My guest explained the pressure they'd been put under. "We have been told the only way we can enter the European market is to buy this factory. They insisted we have no other way into Europe. That is why we had to come." The higher-ups had given them a stark automotive ultimatum.

"Tell me something." One of the other visitors spoke for the first time. His English was perfect and without any accent. "If you're so important to BMW and VW, then why have you so much unused capacity?"

A really good question.

By the middle of December 2010, only two potential investors were left in the game. Things went quiet. They both seemed to have lost interest. Roth became even more of a bully as his desperation grew. Nothing was moving, and he was being blamed for the inactivity.

One Friday night, I was sitting alone in my office when my phone rang. It was Karin Degler.

"I know it's getting late, but we need you to work on some reports." The nice before the nasty—she didn't wait for any response.

"I want the last two years of casting history on every Porsche and BMW part. I need the number of total parts cast and how many of those were good parts. I need to know how many machines were used and how many people to make them. I also want to know…" She continued to rattle off her list of requests, one after another. It became clear she was trying to model the factory and see just what it could do if they pushed it hard before closing it down. That goal had taken precedence over Roth's stated intention of selling the factory. At least he would be seen to be doing something.

When Degler finished her command, I started to fish for my own information. "This is quite some request, Karin. It'll take a week. Is next Friday okay?"

She sounded genuinely frightened. "No!" she shrilled. She paused and tried to regain her composure. "I must have these by Monday morning. Mr. Roth has to present them to the board." She trailed off, realizing she'd shared too much.

She had. Judging by her fear, Roth had been insistent. Obviously he'd been ordered to get this information by someone more senior—perhaps the CEO of Porsche or even higher. The sales process was stalling, so Farsund would definitely be a topic for the next VW board meeting.

I used math and science to show Porsche would still run out of parts quickly if we were closed. We just couldn't make a large enough stockpile. It wasn't a new message, but it was a new audience. Roth was the only way I could communicate with them. He carried their message to me, and I'd answer them through him. The fact they kept asking the same questions really meant they hadn't given up the slaughter option. I had to find something else, another reason that would stop them from trying to close us; something to stop this threat.

***

I also had to find something to help me keep my sanity—a complete distraction from Roth. Nestled in the heart of Farsund was my solution: a bar that once functioned as a thriving community center. It had closed down a long time ago but still existed as a nostalgic reminder of the past for people who had grown up here. It was where they watched their first concert, where they first got drunk, and where they met their first true love.

The building had seen multiple lives, serving at various times as a monastery, church, tobacco shop, hardware shop, toy store, and, most recently, as one of southern Norway's must-see rock pubs. It dated back to the 1750s when, rumor had it, a grateful Russian Tsar gifted it to Farsund as thanks for protecting and sheltering a ship's crew caught in the frozen sea. It afforded a spectacular view of Farsund's harbor, just feet from the quay.

Once cherished but now neglected, it had not been repaired for many years. But it still held a mythical charm. I'd reached a point of desperation to find a distraction and just bought the pub on a whim. There was very little reason behind it; just instinct to be Farsund. But it became my sanctuary. It was where I always spent my time away from the factory.

"I'm afraid we're not open." Dressed in my workwear and holding a paintbrush, I readied myself to thwart any hopeful and thirsty customers. For the past few hours, I had been working on the inside of the second floor.

"Not even for a willing volunteer?" Marit stood at the rear door of the bar. I looked down from the balcony and saw her dressed in overalls suitable for the current surroundings. "I'm quite good at painting," she continued persuasively.

I didn't know she was coming. Normally Hilde would show up, always with a gift. Sometimes it was a flask of coffee, or sometimes it was lunch. This time Hilde's mother was the gift, here to keep me company while I renovated my new project. I certainly could use her help. We spent the next three hours painting.

Finally we stopped for a coffee break, sitting on the stairs with cups in our hands. She asked me, "Exactly why did you buy this place?"

I thought for a moment. "Well, what guy doesn't want his own pub?" I was being flippant. It didn't work. She wasn't going to let it go.

"No, really. You do enough work at the factory. Now you've got this. When do you take time for yourself?" She meant time with Hilde.

"I don't need time for myself. This is my down time. It's a distraction. I'm safe here." I wanted to tell her how much I loved her daughter, but I knew I couldn't reconcile Hilde and my children. I wanted to tell her soon it would be over. Roth would find a way to remove me. But no one needed to know how fragile my high-stakes game had become. Farsund depended on my staying focused. The bar enabled me to block out any kind of feeling. I didn't have time to think about my guilt, love, or joy. I only thought about saving the factory or fixing the bar.

I'm glad I had that pub to work on as the year came to a close. Paint brushes were my Christmas tree, masking tape my decorations, and a sledgehammer my entertainment. I missed my kids but ignored the pain.

***

We exited the grand building, roofed by seven huge, fan-like structures, all in the iconic silver color that reminded me exactly where I was: the heart of innovation, the center of the future; Mercedes' illustrious design building. This was where new cars were created. It was the start of a new year.

Karsten was smiling, something I hadn't seen in a while. "Nice, boss. Very nice." Just a few minutes before, we'd been standing around a design table in the large open atrium, deep in session and trying to build a future. The Mercedes team was composed of three of their best design engineers and two from their purchasing department.

The engineers had been convinced Farsund could do things no other could. They wanted us to make their designs a reality. The purchasing duo remained reluctant. "Who owns you?" one repeated over and over. "You must have financial stability. How can you do that only months after bankruptcy?" Then his colleague chimed in, "How do you get your money?" He'd done the math. It didn't add up.

I held their gaze and, in a slow deliberate tone, said, "I have been told under no circumstances can I share this information with you." At the same time, I opened my briefcase and slid out a sheet of paper. I'd printed it from VW's corporate web page. It showed all the subsidiaries in their empire.

It had taken me hours of searching, but here it was. "Of course, public information is, well, public." I laid the paper on the table and pointed at one line. It named Farsund Aluminium Casting as a subsidiary of Porsche and therefore VW. It was exactly the one thing that would satisfy their skepticism. We couldn't be more stable.

All five looked a little amazed. "Let me check this out," the first purchasing guy said. "If it's real, then congratulations."

We'd won a new contract, the start of many. By the beginning of May 2011, we had five new orders for parts going into Mercedes's new S and C class cars—a future.

Roth left the latest board meeting at about the same time Mercedes placed its biggest order with Farsund. His attempts to sell the factory had stalled again. Benteler International, the only remaining party that had any interest at all, had asked for too much. It wasn't just a revenue thing. That could be solved. They wanted everything. They wanted the factory and all the equipment. They wanted an order book stuffed full. They wanted to keep the open checkbook contracts in place. And to top it all, they wanted $80 million. They said they needed it to invest in new machines. Yeah right!

VW couldn't accept Benteler's offer without further damage to their reputation. It would be a story everyone in the industry would learn and perhaps use if they ever faced a similar situation. It made VW's decision easy: shut down the factory rather than sell it. Finally, BMW would get revenge. And so would Roth.

I'd exhausted my old defense. They weren't listening to logic. I needed something new; something they were more scared of. Mercedes had given me inspiration. I had used VW's ownership to win Mercedes' commitment. Could I reverse that equation?

***

"I do see this time you're serious. I do understand you are all unified in your decision." I was standing in a random meeting room somewhere in Roth's empire, staring down at my shoes. He wanted to witness my reaction as he relayed the unanimous decision to close the factory. My role would apparently be to fulfill their desire and execute my team.

Then I looked up at him and sprang my trap. "We have five new contracts with Daimler. We are legally committed to develop and supply them with these new parts. All are exclusive to us too." He fixed his eyes on me as I spoke in a steady, even tone.

"What did they say when you told them you were going to close the factory down?" I asked. His face didn't move, but his eyes dropped down. His mouth was open and ready to speak. I didn't let him.

"Some of those contracts are for parts they could move easily, but a couple would be really hard to find someone else. It'll screw up their launch plans." The penny was dropping. "They do know. Don't they?"

He still said nothing. Of course Mercedes knew VW was Farsund's ultimate owner. That's why they'd agreed to these contracts, as insurance. If Farsund screwed up, Mercedes would kick VW. If Farsund was closed, VW would end up having to compensate Mercedes with billions of dollars. It was my same reliable strategy, amplified: Take advantage of the bigness of these bullies to limit their power. Porsche had kept BMW to the open checkbook contracts for many years. now I was using Mercedes to police Porsche and VW.

Once again, Roth found himself cornered: He had to carry this message all the way back to the VW board, as well as to BMW.

Naturally, his message didn't go over well. Two weeks later he was back in Farsund with Degler again by his side. This time, though, he was also accompanied by his lawyer and two Porsche consultants. He could no longer rely on the facts I'd given him. Instead, Porsche's consultants were there to plan how to build up enough parts before the factory closed down. The lawyer had a different purpose.

"Show me why you think you have authority to sign on behalf of this company," Roth's lawyer said in a firm, professional voice. He wanted to find a way to make the Mercedes contracts void.

"This is our agreement. You can see both Mr. Roth and I have full authority to sign. It's part of our ownership agreement. I still own 30 percent of this company." I had cut off one of the lawyer's main arguments prematurely.

I continued, "But anyway, that's not how Mercedes' contracts work. They don't need a signature. They work the same way as your contracts work, and BMW's, actually. We make an offer, Mercedes accepts, and if no one changes anything, it becomes a contract after about two weeks—no signature needed. The last one matured yesterday."

Ultimately, Roth returned to Stuttgart with nothing. His lawyer couldn't help him. I'd used Mercedes as a weapon— mutually assured destruction again. His consultants came up empty-handed too. They confirmed my logic. There was no way to build enough parts to get them out of this mess. They would cut themselves off if they tried.

Roth's visit did have two consequences. It pushed the VW board to instruct him to engage with Benteler again and get the factory sold. The gifts Benteler wanted would be much cheaper than starting a fight with Mercedes. Roth didn't seem to care anymore. It felt to me like he'd forgotten his principal value: to guard what he believed in. From this point on, his only objective appeared like it was to make me fail. That was the second consequence.

CHAPTER 29

Shattering Point

———

JULY TO SEPTEMBER 20, 2011

"Are you awake, darling?" No response. I was talking to a door. Behind that door was a bedroom—Victoria's bedroom in her Norwegian home; the first time she'd seen it. It seemed her new life overwhelmed her. Benjamin and Hugo were happy and settled in instantly. This was their second holiday. They had friends to play with and a summer full of adventures just waiting for them. I always saw them smiling and laughing.

Victoria was different. She didn't like the changes in her life. She could ignore them when she was at her real home, back in Annapolis. She could pretend everything remained the same. Dad was just traveling. He wasn't gone. Mum and Dad were still together. But here in Farsund, she couldn't hide from the reality Mum and Dad had built very different lives. Unable to cope with it, she spent much of her time secluded in her bedroom, sleeping the summer away.

The more I tried to get Victoria to come out of her sanctuary, the more she withdrew. She wasn't rejecting me, just the world I'd built. But summer was racing past, and I couldn't slow it down. This was my one chance to be with my most precious people. I just had no idea how to pull Victoria from her shell, one I had made her create.

Time slipped away before I could figure it out. Victoria stood at the airport security gate, bound for America. She looked at me one last time, her eyes puffy from crying. Then she glanced down and said in a soft, cuddly voice, "Don't be sad, Daddy. I love you." She hugged me hard. I'd used that same voice when I nursed her as a small child, when she'd fallen off her bike or gotten stung by a bee. It broke my heart.

My three darlings were gone. One showed her pain. The other two hid theirs. I was to blame in either case.

Before taking them to the airport, I'd scoured the house, room by room, trying to remove any traces of their presence. I knew what I'd return to. I'd done this before. My fantasy this would be their home had ended, so when I returned, the house had to be sterile. I couldn't see a single thing that would remind me of the fun we'd enjoyed over the summer. Any single memento would focus my attention on those memories and lead to a deep sadness. I figured I could overcome my longing to be with them as long as I never thought about it. I had double-checked every room: strictly functional without a hint of love anywhere.

I'd missed something. It waited for me, ready to penetrate my internal defenses. Victoria had fashioned a long white shoelace into the shape of a heart. It sat on one of the chairs in my living room. She hadn't been able to talk to me through most of her visit, but here she was sending me a message. *I love you, Daddy.* I couldn't move it. She was still in my house, what I wanted more than anything. But I had a war to return to, so I blocked her and the boys from my thoughts.

In public, I appeared calmer than ever to veil the emotions that kept leaking out in private. I did everything I could think of to just keep going. I ran for miles every day, harder and harder up every hill. I burned through money like logs on a fire. I downed wine like water. Maybe one of these outlets would afford me some reprieve when I wasn't fighting to save the factory. Maybe it was good in theory, but impossible in reality.

On Monday, September 12, Roth summoned me again to a lifeless meeting room in Frankfurt Airport. I prepared myself to be fired, even bringing a letter of resignation in my briefcase. In fact, this was something I kept with me whenever I met with Roth. It made me feel like I had a get-out plan.

Benteler was back. Furious negotiations, reports, and meetings were ongoing between them, VW, and BMW. Benteler wanted just as much information from me as Roth did and seemed poised for victory.

That's why this time, Roth and I were not alone. Two others from Benteler were present: Christian Theissing and one of his team. Theissing was a sharp corporate guy who'd been assigned the job of buying my factory. Everyone assembled in front of me shared this single-minded purpose.

Theissing broached the topic first: "So Mr. Cockroft, the real question is, are you prepared to sell us your stake in the company? We want to buy all your machines too. Will you do this?"

Roth sat silently, watching my every move. Would I reject the concept? Would I counter? Was I just greedy?

They all braved the busy airport and returned to their various homes. None of them cared this was one of the last summer weekends left to enjoy. They'd achieved their objective and had to report back to their seniors. The deal was on: Cockroft would sell.

I had no options to return home. By the time the meeting ended, I could only stay at the airport hotel. I sat there in the lounge with a whiskey in hand, just trying to soak in what had just transpired. The bar was full, but I didn't see a single person.

Benteler and VW had agreed to a plan, with Roth as their spokesman. VW would give Benteler the factory and all the machines. They'd even get a big bag of cash. I'd insisted VW give Benteler an order book full of new work. They agreed to that too. It meant the factory was safe and Farsund secure. I'd done my job. It also meant I'd be a multi-millionaire, somewhere in the region of $6 million.

It partly came as a relief, especially after years of fanatical attacks and sly maneuvering. It felt as if I'd been fighting the armies of both BMW and VW, deep in the trenches and covered in ditch water. Now, I'd finally done it. I had no bullets left, but my flag still flew high overhead. Farsund was going to be okay, and my family would be more than safe.

The news also unleashed a reaction I simply didn't expect. Part of me despised that money. Now I knew the deal was going to happen, I allowed myself to truly look at who I'd become. The door of my trunk room, deep inside my mind, swung aside. The locks on every trunk shattered into smithereens, and the lids burst open. Even those from my childhood burst open.

In a few months I wouldn't be needed anymore. What would I do? I surveyed the shattered pieces of my life. It was a mess. I'd screwed up a twenty-two-year marriage. I'd abandoned my children. I refused to adopt Hilde's family, yet I loved her. I'd done everything I promised myself I would never do. I also knew the fight with Roth wasn't over, not by any means. He had no intention of making me rich, not with money he'd have to again beg his board for. He already hated me, and this new development only intensified his hatred. Meanwhile, BMW and VW would also want to humiliate me in order to regain some respect. But I couldn't just leave on the next flight out. The future of Farsund, every employee at the factory, depended on this deal. I was stuck there until the deal closed.

Sitting in the airport hotel lounge, I felt overcome with an intense and unbearable pain. The contents from each trunk had spilled out by now and seemed to unite into a loud and howling scream. So loud I couldn't hear anything else.

Desperate to find a reprieve from my guilt, I looked for therapy. I made it to the weekend. Then I decided to go shopping in a furniture store on Saturday, September 17. *Focus on building out my pub.* FAC rented the house I lived in, so I'd be homeless when the deal closed. At least I could put together some kind of nest on my pub's third floor.

"I just need a few things," I said to the store assistant as I nodded toward the aisle.

The assistant dutifully followed as I strode through the furniture store. "I'll take twelve of those chairs and that pine table. Wait, does it extend?" He confirmed it did. "Good, I'll take that too then." I swiftly moved on as he tried to keep up and scrawl down notes.

By the end, I'd ordered two sofas, four sideboards, an oversized desk and chair, a massive bed and two nightstands, several coffee tables, bookshelves, lamps, and a large dining room table and a dozen chairs—all matching with a beautiful teak finish.

"That was fun," the assistant said with a smile as he processed the paperwork.

"Really?" I was surprised. It had given me no pleasure at all.

Actually, it just made me feel worse and even more hollow inside. Outside, rain poured down heavily. The sun was setting behind a blanket of thick gray clouds. I slid into my car and drove back to Farsund, completely disconnected from any physical feeling.

I needed to isolate myself in my rental house for another Saturday night. *Fill the void with noise.* I decided to drink wine and watch the comedy film *Grown Ups*—anything to make me laugh before I fell asleep. But I didn't even finish. I couldn't stand the characters with their kids and perfect lives, smiling, having fun, being happy, solving their problems. They were taunting me.

I couldn't take the torture of being alone and far away from my children. But I couldn't leave Farsund without screwing up everything. And even if I did leave, I didn't have anywhere else to go. Guilt overwhelmed me with pain as its reward. It wasn't a dull throbbing pain. This was a full-scale, intense screaming pain. I felt I was soaked in sulfuric acid, melting my skin, burning my face off, dissolving my soul. The only logical choice was to stop it. I finally understood why my mum had done what she did.

I sent a text to Hilde saying that I hated myself. Then I turned off my phone and went out into the hallway. Dark thoughts had crept into my mind for some time, but I had ignored them along with everything else. When you start having these types of feelings, you go through the process and visualize how you'd do the physical act of killing yourself. You reason that this isn't ever going to happen, but just for a hypothetical exercise, you work out the details. It felt kind of therapeutic, like my resignation letter. I didn't intend to use it, but it was comforting to know that I had an escape plan.

Victoria had been given a red dog leash from the vet to thank her for her summer work. It was one of those mementos left behind, discarded on the dining room table. I hadn't moved it since she left it there. Perhaps I had subconsciously saved it for this very moment. I picked it up and climbed the stairs in the hallway. I used it to lash a noose to the balcony rails on the second floor. Halfway up the stairs, I put the noose around my neck and stepped over the banister rail. Perched on the outside step, I prepared myself. I looked through the front door window. I saw my Porsche, lit by the hallway light. *Ironic that's the last thing I'm going to see*, I thought. It was as if Roth was there, watching me.

Thousands of screaming and spiteful voices in my head kept chanting the same thing, "Do it! Do it!" It felt as though I was suspended above my own body, looking down at myself, an utter failure.

I couldn't take the final step. I just couldn't. In disgrace, I climbed back over the banister rail and sat on the stairs with the noose still around my neck and my head in my hands. The voices didn't stop screaming. They were angry they'd been robbed of a soul. They urged me to pull against the noose so I could feel what it would be like to have a tightened rope around my neck.

I followed orders. Suddenly, I could see them, little black blobs with bright white eyes, all full of glee. Clever little dark demons, they'd tricked me. They'd gotten one.

I don't remember anything after that. I guess I must have passed out as the noose got to work.

Hilde didn't like my text. It wasn't the first time either. I'd repeatedly told her how much I hated myself. This time, though, she sensed an intensification of the pattern. She couldn't reach me, no matter how many times she tried. My phone was switched off. Her dread grew. She begged her neighbor to watch her children and then drove through the rain to my house as fast as she could.

It had been fifteen minutes since the dark demons had taken me. Hilde looked through the door window and saw me slumped at the bottom of the stairs. She thought I was just sitting there, and then she realized I was hanging. My tongue was black, and my face was blue. Luckily she had a key to get inside. She tried to lift me, but my dead weight made me too heavy. Dashing into the kitchen, she found a sharp knife to cut me down.

I fell to the floor, unconscious. Hilde pulled the noose off my neck and rang the emergency services. They were there in five minutes. My childhood taught me those types of minutes are the longest and most hellish. I was hardly breathing but making noises Hilde later described as "coming from the devil himself."

The paramedics stabilized me in about an hour before they could move my body. The rain and wind prevented them from using a helicopter to airlift me. The only option was to take the road to Kristiansand Hospital, ninety minutes away. About twenty minutes later, my situation deteriorated. Now any hospital would be better than watching me die in the back of an ambulance. They made the decision to turn around for Flekkefjord instead, still forty minutes away.

A miracle happened as we dashed through the endless tunnels skirting the massive fjords. Some combination of drugs worked. I started to regain a faint slice of consciousness. I was tethered to a gurney, with wires and tubes coming out of me. I couldn't move, and my right hand was strapped across my body. The only light I could make out was the dull red glow of the ambulance. *Is this a nightmare?* I suddenly heard myself screaming as I tried to break free. The doctor leaned down into my face and shouted to try to break into my mind. This worked because for a moment I stopped thrashing about.

He asked me what my name was. I told him, but the red light made him look evil. I could have been bound in hell. Fear overcame me, and I started to thrash about again. The doctor had to sedate me. As I slipped into an uneasy calm, I heard him say in English, "We got him back."

My eyes opened slowly. I wasn't tethered anymore but lying on a stretcher. Slowly I focused, and what I thought was one bulb became a collection of bright strip lights recessed into the ceiling. I kept staring, but I couldn't recognize them. *Where am I?* I felt as if I were floating. *Maybe this is heaven?*

Then I heard a voice. A head appeared in my field of view: a man; then a second, this one a woman. Both were dressed in blue scrubs.

"Do you know who you are? Do you know what happened?"

I didn't have a clue. I just kept asking, "Is this a dream? Is this real?" then they would softly repeat in unison what I had said, as though it confirmed some suspicion they had.

I looked down at my body lying flat on the stretcher. I wanted to figure out where I was. Any clue would help me. I saw myself wearing a green gown and strange, string-netted underwear. Other than that I was completely naked. But I wasn't cold. It was a warm place.

Gradually, snippets of what had happened came back to me. The last thing I could recall was sitting on the staircase back home with a noose around my neck. But I struggled with a huge gap in my memory. They asked me what had caused this to happen.

"Did you take any drugs?" the man said.

"No. I don't do drugs," I said definitively.

"Have you been drinking then?"

"Yes. I drank some wine."

The woman took a note.

He reeled off a list of possible triggers, looking for something that could have landed me here.

"How are your relationships?" he finally asked.

"Oh god." I sighed. "My life is a mess." I remembered it all now. It was back.

"Do you want anyone to speak to?" the woman asked.

I just whimpered, "I need Hilde," and then started to cry.

My memory of that night gets blurry from there. At one point, the doctors got Hilde on the phone, but I don't fully recall what I said to her. The next thing I knew, she was there by my side. I had been moved into a room, and they had set up a bed for her next to me. I had tubes and wires attached to my arm and chest, so I could barely move. They must have given me something pretty strong because I felt exhausted and in a daze. Hilde held my hand again and was just there for me. She didn't judge or question. I didn't deserve her.

After a while I needed the bathroom. I wheeled my stand of attachments out of the room and into the corridor, looking for the loo. It was then I realized we were in the ICU. I felt so guilty taking up a bed that should have been available for someone really sick. How selfish of me to waste these good people's time.

At dawn, I got out of bed and checked myself in the mirror. I had a big mark stretching around my neck. The skin was broken in places but mostly intact. The mark was about a half-inch wide and all shades of red before fading out to light-yellow bruises around the fringes. It was my ugly albatross, and I had to wear it shamefully.

Overwhelmed by what I'd done, I returned to my bed. I needed to talk to my brother. We'd shared every bad moment together, and I needed to tell him what had happened. The nurse let me use my phone. But when Dave picked up, I wasn't sure what to say. What were any of us going to get from that call?

"Dave, are you sitting down? Yes, well, I tried to kill myself last night, and I'm in hospital now. No, I'm fine, no problem at all." It sounded so false, like I was telling him I had a cold. I didn't deserve his sympathy. I just wanted to hear his voice. I asked he didn't tell anyone, not even his wife. Then Hilde took the phone, and they talked for some time as she filled him in on the details. They agreed to touch base daily until things got back to normal.

Dave cried a little, and then we cried together. This all felt eerily familiar. Once he had composed himself, he finally said, "Rog, you've got to change your life. I need you, brother."

They moved me to the wardroom and told me I needed to stay there for the night so they could perform an ultrasound to check if I had damaged my arteries. That couldn't be done until Monday. I suggested I could just come back, but then I realized I was also there under observation. In fact, I wasn't allowed out until I'd been released following a psychiatric evaluation.

Hilde was with me for as long as she could but then left with the promise to return. I'm not sure how she managed it, but she must have just dumped the kids with her neighbors and shot out the door. She'd stayed with me all night and well into the next morning.

When she left, I slept or wandered around the hospital day room, trying to be as inconspicuous as possible. I wasn't very successful. At one point a few nurses gathered outside my room. One poked her head in and said, "Oh, it's you. How's the new pub doing in Farsund?" The last thing I wanted was to be recognized. I felt ashamed by what I'd done and didn't want anyone to know about it, especially not Roth. This was exactly what they wanted. They would tear me to pieces if they found out. So I stayed in my room and out of the way. Occasionally I'd get up and take a look at the noose mark around my neck, but then I'd lie back on the bed and get lost in a fog of thoughts. Sunday slipped away.

Monday morning came, and the hospital burst back into life. After an all-clear from the ultrasound department, I went back to my room to wait for the psychiatrist. I needed to get back to work. I started answering emails on my phone. I told my management team I had a medical issue and wouldn't be in but didn't elaborate more. I fielded several demanding calls from Degler who seemed angry I wasn't in my office. I assured her I would be back on Tuesday and answered her questions. Life was going to proceed as usual, and I would have to be stronger now.

Hilde turned up again and apologized to me. Apparently to be allowed in she had told the desk staff she was my partner, and she was worried about how I would react. This is the woman who had saved my life, dropped everything, and never once judged me but just offered comfort and support. And here she was apologizing for loving me. I don't think she has ever fully understood I love her just as much. Denying yourself the love you feel will eventually get you in trouble.

She'd packed some fresh clothes for me. I wore a high-necked black sweater that just about covered the noose marks. I still felt self-conscious and kept tugging the sweater up.

When the psychiatrist finally arrived, I was surprised to see she was the mother of one of my loyal engineers, Rune Svestol. I knew he trusted me and had only stayed with the company because of his trust. Of course, she was bound by confidentiality and too professional to share patients' cases with her family, but her presence made me realize how interrelated this whole community was. Everyone had a job to do. That's how it survived. I had a job to do, too, and people had put their faith in me. I couldn't do this again. I had to be better.

I was discharged on Monday afternoon, less than two days after my suicide attempt. The hospital staff gave me a series of numbers I could call if I felt weak again. I convinced myself I wouldn't need them.

On Tuesday, September 20, I returned to work. I had a mountain of emails to catch up on. I also had to go into the factory and help with the new trial parts we were casting. My team needed my moral support to complete the difficult job I'd asked of them. No one could know my terrible secret. I kept my neck covered all week with high-necked sweaters, though I only had two or three of them and worried people would call me out for wearing the same thing twice.

I had to accept I still faced the same situation. I couldn't move forward with Hilde until I could find a way of being with my kids too. Meanwhile, I needed to be strong enough to live with my loneliness until I'd finished my job. After all, I had committed myself to this community. They had confidence in me that I didn't have in myself.

Now was not the time to fail.

The blackest of black days

Your mind gets pretty sly
When the time finally comes to die
Your mind quickly creates
Deathly self-hates
What's the point of airs and graces?
When the noose is all that your neck faces

*

I should have been stronger
I should have fought
But now everything is so distraught
I can't hope, I can't hate
I just know that this is my fate

*

The moment's here
The time has come
Make your peace and forget what you've done
Take your last look
Think your last thought
This is the future that your money bought

*

Can you hear the million voices shouting all the same?
They don't care about your name
They shout "do it, do it" again and again
The cacophony is so loud you can't stand the pain
Forget the ones you love and who love you
Just do what you're compelled to do
Anything to stop the pain of being you

*

There's no pain
There's nothing, mad or sane

It's just black without feeling
It's not like you get a sense of healing
Waste, just waste, if anything
But you feel just a taste

*

I still haven't figured what was worse?
Waking with the shame of what I did
Or waking knowing I cheated the hearse

CHAPTER 30

Guilt Is an Emotion

SEPTEMBER 25, 2011 TO MARCH 29, 2012

I felt exhausted even though plenty of hours remained in the day. I was so exhausted that I struggled to stand up. I crumpled over and burst into tears. But these weren't tears of either sadness or euphoria. They were tears of determination.

At that moment, as I crossed the finish line of the Berlin Marathon, I made a pact with myself. I couldn't let myself consider suicide ever again. Someone placed a medal around my neck. The red, yellow, and black ribbon contrasted against the fading bruises. I knew I had to find my inner strength to live up to my promises. I just didn't know how.

At first, it proved easier to fall back on my old ways, not realizing how much I had taken a page from my enemies' playbook. I resolved to be ruthless like Roth—a fortress. I felt he never allowed weakness to fool him. I continued to see emotion as a weakness. So I decided to do terrible things to prove I could ignore emotion. Guilt is an emotion, I reasoned. I had to become impervious to guilt.

Hilde became the target of my newfound callousness, even after all she'd done for me. I perceived the joy her love gave me just made me weak. It made me lose focus, so I had to shut her love out. I wanted her to reject me. Then she would feel it was her decision to leave me. If she saw me with other women, I'd give her the very reason to ditch me. I owned the local bar, and it wouldn't be hard to find suitable candidates, but it didn't work. Somehow, she forgave me for betraying and humiliating her. So I upped the ante.

"Good night, sir," I said with a very polite English accent as I shook the man's hand while I was lying in my bed. He was the last guest who would leave the room.

It was 3:00 a.m. and the end of an extravagant party on the top floor of my pub, the penthouse suite. I'd overpoured the wine all night until everyone was tipsy. Then I'd enticed one of the guests to an oversized bed in the corner of the penthouse. Now we were both under the sheets and naked from the waist down.

Hilde was left alone, sitting at the dinner table. She had seen everything I'd done.

I'd put Hilde in a horrible situation, a scene I'd composed where she would have to witness my misdeeds. I'd abandoned all of my values to try and prove two things: prove to myself I was absolutely ruthless, and prove to Hilde I was not someone she wanted to be with. Surely this would give her the motivation to break up and leave me.

It didn't work either. Hilde couldn't let me go. If she reacted negatively in any way, she would have to leave me. She didn't. She joined us.

I have never forgiven myself for what I did that night. I wish I could apologize to all of these people I manipulated and disrespected. I did learn something, though. I learned I was not and could not be a self-destructive, soulless man. I could not betray true love. Guilt has a purpose. Feelings guide a soul. Honesty and trust are virtues. These emotions were not my enemies. I knew who my real enemies were.

***

I couldn't believe it. We'd done it. I was overwhelmed as I was offered the trophy. I desperately thought what to say. "I'd like to thank all those people who voted for us." The spotlights blinded my view of the hundreds of audience members. I stood on the stage in the NTNU Studentersamfundet, or Red Round Building. Jan Ove and Per Erik stood next to me, ecstatic. As graduates from that university, they could not have been more proud to be there, finally gaining recognition for their abilities.

We had won the national Award for Engineering Innovation, one of Norway's most prestigious honors. "One vote for every email account, huh!" I joked. "I now have fourteen new email addresses." The audience laughed but not with much conviction. I was holding the trophy, a sophisticated circle of interweaved cogs on a plinth. I handed it to Jan Ove who turned to Norwegian and engaged the crowd.

It was more than just an award. New business was flooding into the factory. Even BMW had given us a bigger share of their demand for all the parts we made for them. Jaguar Land Rover had given us business for their F type and the new Range Rover. And with the Mercedes contracts, we now had eleven new large orders and a bright future. Farsund finally found itself on the path toward growth and recovery.

But we still needed greater publicity. Roth had banned me from spending money to recruit new talent I so desperately needed to deliver on the promises of all these new orders. And it wasn't just me. The entire community of Farsund was recovering from the recession. Others were recruiting too.

I asked for a meeting with Richard Buch, the new mayor, to talk about our plans to grow the factory. In return, he invited his executive team. We sat around a large table in his personal meeting room deep in the Husan historical building. The grand town hall had been rebuilt in 1901 after a fire razed it to the ground.

"I can live anywhere, as long as it's Farsund," I quipped to Buch. Then I began telling him about my idea to get Farsund to advertise on our behalf.

"Let's make a series of ads. We can put them in all the national papers; invite people to come look; put up a website too. We can post any openings we have."

Buch nodded and wore a smile. "We've got new wind in our sails now," he said. With spring approaching, they all believed things would only get better.

The campaign worked. Within a few months I watched new people join our team, not only from Norway, but also from Germany, Spain, and even as far as Brazil. We smuggled them under the radar. Roth saw nothing.

***

On March 29, 2012, the taxi driver dropped me off at the curb of Porsche Platz. I'd been called to another meeting with Roth. Roth's assistant took me to a room and then opened a well-worn, brown door. I stood behind her.

I immediately saw six occupants, fully engaged and leaning into the table: Herald Hoschek, Peter Gaehrken, and Joachim Goldbach from BMW; and Martin Roth, Karin Degler, and Stephen Spreiter from VW/Porsche. Hoschek was talking and pointing at a computer screen. He continued to talk as his head turned to the door. At first, he saw only Roth's assistant, but then he noticed me. His words fizzled out as a look of bewilderment formed. He stopped mid-sentence. Everyone else followed his stare.

"Good morning, everyone," I said with vim in my tone. "My, you all look busy."

Roth shouted in German to his assistant, "Not in here! Take him to my office!" He didn't want me to know of this meeting.

Roth's assistant looked distraught as she rushed me out of the room and down the corridor to Roth's office. The room was small and crammed full of reports, books, and cardboard boxes. An undersized circular meeting table was squeezed into the corner, with just enough room for three chairs. His desk was so cluttered you could barely find room to park a coffee cup. I looked out of the dingy window. It overlooked the central courtyard, with red brick walls on every side—not an inspiring view.

Minutes later, Roth walked in. His assistant begged her apology. He brushed her aside and took his seat behind the desk. Degler dutifully followed, clutching a folder full of files. She took a seat opposite his desk. There was just the perfect amount of space to place her folder, her usual perch.

"I have made a deal with both BMW and Benteler," he announced proudly. "We will pay Benteler to take over the factory in Farsund." I'd heard Benteler had asked for $82 million. All the big players must have agreed: Dr. Herbert Diess for BMW, Francisco Javier García Sanz for VW, and even Hubertus Benteler, who had deigned to visit Farsund earlier that year. His private jet had made his trip simple. The amount of money he'd get from VW and BMW to take over the factory made his decision even simpler.

"We will have to change the way we structure the deal." Roth was referring to our previous discussion in Frankfurt Airport back in September, right before my suicide attempt. Quickly Degler blurted out, "It's in the best interest of the long-term continuation of the factory." That expression, so overused and empty by now, made me shudder.

"I assume you will negotiate with me for the sale of the assets of the company." His anger from a few minutes earlier had now morphed into cold professionalism. This was a well-prepared script he delivered calmly for once. "FAC, the company, will buy your assets and your 30 percent share directly. In addition, we will give you our 30 percent of your company, Buhive. You don't need to be involved in any of the discussions with Benteler. We have to keep that confidential."

He finished. Both of them stared at me, waiting for my response.

This was good news. It sounded like they were committed. It sounded like this time they were actually prepared to complete the sale. It sounded like the factory did have a future. It was exactly what I wanted.

I composed myself to look calm. Underneath I was giddy with hope. Finally I spoke. "Mr. Roth, I need you to promise your integrity is focused on a fair conclusion of this sale. We've all been through a tremendous mess over the last three years. I will play nice if you do. I want Farsund to have a future." I checked both their expressions. They were waiting for the punch. "Let's try it this way. Let's see if we can do this."

We spent the next twenty minutes talking about deal structures, and then a newly energized Roth did something unusual. For the first time he offered to take the three of us to lunch. Ironically, he chose the same steak restaurant Wiker and I had visited in the famous Porsche Museum three years ago. Everything was exactly the same, including the smells. I couldn't help thinking about what had happened there on my last visit. I had hatched my plan to steal the machines and defend the factory in this place. Now here I was again, about to embark on its final stage. We could all win as long as we played nice.

Something irked me, though. Something didn't feel quite right. I didn't know what it was, but my suspicion lingered. *Maybe I should talk to Wiker*, I thought.

CHAPTER 31

Flip of a Coin

———

APRIL TO OCTOBER 12, 2012

Wiker tilted back in his chair and put his hands behind his head. We were sitting in his office in Oslo.

"Ahhh, Roger!" He sighed. "So you had lunch in that restaurant again. Did you? I hope you had something bigger than your favorite lady steak."

Then he leaned forward and picked up a magazine lying on his desk. "I came across an interesting article. It's an interview with Mr. Roth." He began to read it aloud.

"He says he can identify weak suppliers and always takes *appropriate measures*." Wiker emphasized these last two words. "Then he goes on to say he will always terminate business relationships if you are a risk to Porsche, and he does it quickly."

Wiker went on, making himself very clear. "Oh, this is a good one. Here he says he never restructures or puts money into companies. It's fundamentally unacceptable to him and to Porsche."[1]

He tossed the magazine back onto his desk and reclined in his chair again. "Look what he's done: divide and conquer. He'll keep you guessing."

Wiker looked me straight in the eyes now and said his next words with special gravity. "Prepare yourself, Roger. Be ready. He's coming for you." I felt like a fool.

It took just a week until Wiker was proved right. I was in Hamburg for Easter weekend with my two boys. It was a short visit, but I'd take any moment I could have with them. I'd combined several business meetings with a road trip. We'd checked into a hotel on the banks of the river Elbe, overlooking the massive aircraft manufacturing factory across the banks.

"Wow, Pa! That man was really angry. Do they all shout like that?" Benjamin, my older son, had overheard the call I'd just finished with Roth.

"Not everyone, but Mr. Roth is a special case, unfortunately." I'd just endured another thirty-minute rant. It had gone exactly the way Wiker predicted. He told me I had to give him the machines. If I didn't, he'd set his lawyers on me, he'd bankrupt the company, he'd publicly shame me, and he'd make sure every single person in my factory was told it was my fault, right before he sacked them.

Roth had issued an ultimatum and given me the Easter weekend to decide. I sat with both boys in our hotel room on the edge of the bed and explained the situation, including the perilous state of the factory and Roth's relentless threats.

With Benj and Hugo on either side of me, I asked, "What do you think I should do?"

Benj summed it up, "You taught us to never give in, especially not to bullies." I felt a mixture of pride in my children and resignation I must follow my own words. The end game was in play. Roth had a strategy and full support from his superiors. He had resources too—endless resources.

He swooped in with his next move the second I rejected his demand. I had to field calls from the local press before I even got back to Farsund. All of them were demanding an answer to the same question: "Is it true you are moving the factory to Poland?" Roth had clearly learned how to communicate with the community through the press.

I met with the reporters to quash this rumor. I assured them the factory had a full order book and a bright future. Farsund would always be its home. My promise made front-page headlines the next morning.

The following day I got a phone call from Karsten Mohr. "Boss, Mercedes just told me they have changed our contracts. Now they've given them to Benteler, but insisted their parts have to be made in Farsund."

Someone had done something very clever and devious. I suspect it was Roth. Benteler's name was now on all the contract agreements with Mercedes, not FAC. Although Mercedes still wanted FAC to make the parts, there was no agreement between FAC and either Benteler or Mercedes. Instantly, Porsche and VW were off the hook. I couldn't use Mercedes as a threat to keep Roth in line anymore.

He ghosted me and cut off my cash. With just pennies in our bank, mid-May was getting ugly. Roth refused to take my calls. I couldn't pay all the company's bills. He found other ways to cut off our cash flow too.

Porsche rejected hundreds of parts we'd already supplied. That meant they didn't have to pay for them. They didn't explain what the problems were, but they insisted those parts had quality problems. Chaos was building in the factory. New customers were screaming for their new parts, suppliers were screaming to get paid, and Porsche was screaming about phantom quality problems. We were on the verge of collapse.

The time had come for him to deliver his message. He had a solution. He could save my team. Benteler could save them. He just didn't want me to hear it. He chose the annual board meeting as his venue—the exact same location where his previous bosses, Wendelin Wiedeking and Holger Härter, had been deposed. Now it would be his turn to depose me.

"Next topic," Roth announced in a dominant tone, as if needing to remind everyone he was chairman of the board. It was Monday, May 21, and the meeting had been going badly for over an hour. Roth had already put all our new contracts on hold and again refused to allow us to buy the tools we needed to make new parts. He had stopped our ability to grow.

He started speaking in German, "Ich möchte mit Ihnen über eine sehr attraktive Gelegenheit sprechen." A woman whom I had never seen before sprang into action as soon as he finished his opening sentence. In Norwegian she said, "I want to talk to you about a very attractive opportunity." She was his translator. Two members of the board were union reps from the factory. He was speaking to them. He knew I didn't speak much Norwegian.

Jan Espland, one of the representatives, looked a little bemused. He leaned across the meeting table, and then restated everything in English for me. He nodded as he did it, all while making eye contact with Roth. A look of frustration crossed Roth's face. He had annotated his presentation in German and Norwegian but now realized Jan would just translate it. Reluctantly, he continued his speech in broken English as his translator quietly sat back down. He didn't say what he wanted them to hear. Roth had to find another way to get his message to the factory.

Despite this failed attempt, Roth really did have his foot on my neck. His superiors at VW, Porsche, and BMW had given him a deadline of June 30 to resolve all issues and put Benteler in charge. We were his embarrassing faux pas, and it was payback time.

He seemed to adopt the same ploy I'd used against him three years ago—except with a vindictive twist. If he could inflict simultaneous bankruptcy on the factory and on Buhive, my company that owned the assets, I would immediately lose control of everything. It would enable him to buy all the machines he wanted for pennies from the bankruptcy administrator. He could just give them to Benteler.

Throughout June, he launched a slew of actions targeted to create chaos and topple Buhive. He threatened the company's dissolution by refusing to sign financial documents. He tried to stop rental payments for the equipment. He kept changing his role as the Porsche representative to Buhive so that any formal communications or meetings couldn't happen.

Meanwhile, he'd taken away my bargaining power and made me invisible to his bosses. I was not included in any negotiations to sell the factory.

As the end of June loomed, I tried hard not to budge. I found ways of recruiting new talent, with the mayor helping to pay for our advertising. My team labored to keep our new customers happy. Somehow they kept making prototype parts from broken tools just when Mercedes needed them. But I was running on fumes.

As far as Benteler was concerned, the deal was already done. They treated FAC like a subsidiary of their empire. They talked to our customers like they were theirs. They were negotiating on our behalf for new contracts. They were directing my team. They visited on a daily basis. To everyone at Benteler it was just the last-minute paperwork holding up the close of the deal. They didn't know Roth was still fighting with me, unwilling to negotiate and putting the company under financial stress.

The ordeal was ugly, and Roth was ruthless. I had no choice but to fight. Farsund was my home. Richard Buch proved it was when the US Ambassador, Barry White, visited the town just days before the Fourth of July. He was there to recognize the deep relationships Farsund had with America. I was one of forty guests invited to the formal welcome dinner at the splendid city hall. I'd become a US citizen in 2010.

After dessert, Mayor Buch stood up and began speaking. "Mr. White—Barry, it is truly an honor you would take time to visit Farsund, especially now, so close to your Independence Day. We have a lot of ties to America. Many of us lived in New York for some part of our life. But tonight I want you to hear from someone who is an English-American and has chosen to live here." Almer Friestad, the industry liaison officer for Farsund, leaned over to me and whispered, "I told him to get you to speak. I hope that's okay."

The mayor continued, "I know I haven't asked him yet, but I'd like to introduce you to Roger Cockroft. He is an upstanding member of our community. He's fought for us. He's brought tremendous value to Farsund, and I'm proud to call him a friend." He then waved his hand toward me. "Roger, would you mind addressing this audience?" The hall filled with applause.

As I stood up, I thought for a moment I'd been blindsided. Then I paused. He had honored me in a way I needed to hear. I only needed to voice my true feelings. So I raised my head and said, "Farsund isn't an easy place to find. It's not exactly big, but its reputation pops up all over the world. I came across it in downtown Las Vegas…" I continued for another five minutes.

"…This town, this community, is as priceless as anywhere you can find. It's full of pure, honest people, who strive for perfection, who care for each other, and who are humble. I'm proud to be American, and I'm equally proud to be here. For me, apparently what happened in Vegas stayed in Farsund." What I said went down well with the audience. These were my friends.

As the dinner wound to an end, Barry walked over and began quizzing me about my history. Then he said to his aide, "Can you arrange Roger to join me tomorrow for lunch? Then I'd like to tour his factory." He shook my hand. "If that's okay with you, Roger." Of course it was.

The following day, I stood with him for the final time in my reception. We'd shared lunch and toured the factory. White shook my hand again. In his palm was an Ambassador Challenge Coin. He firmly pressed it into my hand.

"The mayor chose you as the voice of Farsund last night—impressive. It's more than trust. Whatever you do, whatever it is, keep it up. Don't stop." He left the coin in my hand. I knew then that I had work to do.

"Get me Cockroft. Now!" Roth barked at Elizabeth, our receptionist, before retreating to the customer conference room, his chosen beachhead.

It was the start of Roth's invasion. He'd decreed he would visit Farsund and demanded to talk to the entire team. He planned to reveal I was the bad guy, prepared to sacrifice anyone for my own gain. Christian Theissing and Benteler's Norwegian manager, Strandlie, joined him.

It was Wednesday, July 4, 2012— three years since Roth had signed the cast-iron contracts. In less than a week, he would have to report to Porsche's CEO and board. They would expect him to have already sold FAC to Benteler, the dreadful Farsund saga finished once and for all. He had a deadline. If he could postdate the deal to the end of June then FAC would simply disappear from any VW reports.

Yet Roth didn't feel pressure. This was his plan, and he was ready to execute it. The factory was on the brink of failure, he had a committed buyer, and he had thwarted my threat to use Mercedes against him. Now it was time for his final moves—sweet revenge.

I walked into our customer room. Roth was in his usual spot at the end of the table with just Degler. Theissing and Strandlie had been cast out of the room.

"Consider this a shareholder meeting." Roth grunted, wasting no time. "Either you give me the assets, or I will close the factory down. I will make the company bankrupt."

I answered, "My mind is unchanged. Do what you have to do."

Somehow he managed not to scream. In a low voice he simply said, "The shareholder meeting is over."

Within an hour he had gathered the management team, and the two labor union representatives were there. Theissing and Strandlie made up the quorum.

Roth instantly called the meeting to order. "This factory isn't special. You've all been told many lies." He stared directly at me. "You have one chance of survival. Accept my plan. Let Benteler take control." He knew this would cost Porsche $84 million, and that was in addition to the $80 million I'd already cost him over the last three years. But that didn't matter to him now.

He continued, "Cockroft's shoddy management has driven this company to the point of bankruptcy. Unless you agree to what I want, I will let that happen." The room fell silent.

Then I spoke. "Well that's not true. Is it?" My voice was mild, but my mind was racing. *Of course*, I thought. *I have it. I have the answer. I know what to do.*

"I have been asking for money for three months now. And you've ignored every request. We need another $3 million just to get our bank accounts back to the levels as spelled out in our contractual agreements. My requests are perfectly legitimate to the contracts we all drew up exactly three years ago." I paused.

"And they're still valid. They will be for another two years. So as I see it... we can't go bankrupt. You'll have to pay all our bills. You'll be sued for any commitments the factory reasonably made and can't deliver. You'll be sued for mishandling all the employees. And you'll have to honor these contracts for every minute until they expire."

Silence.

"It will get really ugly. The government will get involved," I looked at the union reps, "and I guess you guys will too." They nodded slightly, enough for Roth to see.

"No! Stop this!" Roth screamed. "I will destroy this factory! It's finished." Degler jumped in and stretched out her hands to try and calm him.

Both the labor union representatives looked at each other and nodded, now convinced of which path to take.

I had one more move left. I would push him over the top with my final comment. "I insist the records show I formally requested funds in line with the agreed contracts and they have been denied by Mr. Roth. I've already told our external auditor, and he agrees with me. We will default next week, and it will be down to you." I stared at Roth.

Roth's face was puffy, his eyes were red, and he looked like he was about to explode. He contained himself just long enough to finish the meeting. My team and I left. I could hear his rage from outside the room. Theissing and Degler were trying to calm him. Strandlie just kept quiet.

At 6:00 p.m. I was ready to go home. I stood outside the customer room—silence. I poked my head in. "I'm leaving for the day. Is there anything else you need from me?"

This was enough to ignite Roth again. "I want nothing from you!" he spat out.

Theissing, who had been nursing Roth up until this point, broke off. He looked at me and said, "Just a moment—I do have something." He pointed to the door. He wanted to talk to me alone.

Theissing followed me into the reception and asked, "Can we meet tonight, please?" We agreed to reunite at the Rederiet Hotell after I'd had time to run. I needed to purge my feelings and reset my emotions.

Farsund shone like a vibrant gem that evening. Eight hundred people were enjoying the music, outdoor bar, and barbecue of a summer concert. I could hear the hubbub from the reception of the hotel foyer. Appropriately, I was sitting in the exact same seat I had used when Wiker and I first met there.

Theissing looked flustered. He couldn't believe how the earlier meeting had transpired. "I have never seen anything like that. He's completely lost control of himself. This has nothing to do with business. This is all about you. It's totally personal. He hates you." Theissing clearly had no idea Roth was going to let the factory go bankrupt. He was seeing for the first time Roth's fixation on pursuing a vendetta.

I replied, "Mr. Roth has always had a tough side, but he let go of his professional concerns about six months ago. He did with me, anyway. He really doesn't care about this factory anymore. He's willing to let it die regardless of the consequences: not to Farsund, not to Porsche or BMW, not even to Benteler."

Theissing frowned when I said Benteler's name. "Not us. It's not our problem. We don't own the factory."

I looked him in the eyes. "Not the factory, no, but you do own the factory's contracts."

It felt to me like Roth hadn't just deceived his own empire. In my mind he'd tricked Benteler too. He apparently had persuaded them to take responsibility for contracts to supply some very complex parts to Mercedes. Mercedes had also agreed to give their contracts to Benteler. Doing this had taken away any liability Porsche had; liability I tried to use to keep my factory open. Theissing realized he was legally on the hook to deliver parts only my factory could make. And meanwhile, Roth seemed to be maneuvering to bankrupt both the factory and Buhive. It would cost Benteler many millions of dollars and much reputation if we closed down.

"He won't get control of Buhive quickly enough. If he forces the factory into bankruptcy again, I will destroy the equipment myself." My message wasn't a threat. It was a statement of fact.

"I need to make some calls," Theissing said. He ended the meeting and rushed up the hotel stairs to his room.

That Wednesday was America's Independence Day. It was also the night we finally celebrated our independence from Roth. He was removed from all discussions. From that moment forth, all emails came from his personal assistant, vetted by VW's lawyers and written by Degler. I never spoke to him again.

The following Monday, we received our much-needed operational funds. BMW and Porsche started complying with those cast-iron contracts again. All communications were either directly with Degler or through emails; all very clinical without personal animosity.

By mid-August, we had settled the deal. Benteler would get the factory and all the equipment. I would get exactly $6 million in return for my assets. The battle ended on Friday, September 7, when, finally, all sales were complete, money was transferred, and the deal closed.

I left Farsund later in October, back to America to build a new life with my kids and my dogs. It had been a five-year experience that was meant to last just three months. I learned the name "Farsund" comes from the Norwegian word for "travel" or "journey." That journey had taken me to places I'd never expected and stretched me past my breaking point, but I had done it. I had gone all the way.

Benteler kept the factory for five years before deciding to sell it to a professional casting company, Aludyne—a huge multinational organization that wants to keep and grow the business (genuinely) for the long-term future. Huge investments in the latest technology have strengthened the company's capabilities. They form an integral part of Europe's automotive supply chain.

One of the last things I saw before leaving Farsund was a swathe of new people from Denmark, Brazil, Spain, and of course Norway taking up new positions in the company and moving into the community. That growth has continued to this day. All two hundred jobs have been reestablished, and another four hundred new jobs have been created in the community. The influx of new talent has spawned new industries, new technology, and new careers. And it's not just the industrial sector that's booming but all sectors: homes, schools, shops, and bars. Because of our success, Farsund now has a truly sustainable platform upon which to flourish.

When the business faced bankruptcy at the end of 2008, our production supervisor, Frank Edvinsen, asked me, "Why are you fighting so hard for us?" He knew I could have just gone home. I replied, "Because I can." That wasn't really the right answer. I should have answered, "Because I should." Farsund and, more specifically, the team deserved everything I could give them; my very best. They were worthy of a better future because they never wavered from their core values.

I didn't know what my own future was when I left. But I could look back at my past and walk away with my head held high in the knowledge I didn't balk when the going got tough. It turned out Farsund gave me my "Geir moment." It's true this cost Porsche and BMW a lot of money—at least $170 million by my estimates, and that doesn't include all the legal fees and other expenses. But they produced every car they wanted to build. They didn't miss a single one. It could have cost them so much more. If they'd have thought, it needn't have cost them a single dime.

It did cost many of their careers, though. Some were told to retire, quietly removed from their posts. Others faced worse. They were assigned a window to stare out from, exactly the fate I'd escaped before coming to Farsund. You may keep your title, even your office, but all responsibilities are stripped from you. All you do is spend day after day gazing out of the same window, at the same, red-bricked, courtyard, looking at all those cars, knowing you have no credibility anymore.

Epilogue

Hilde and I agreed it was time for me to be a dad again. She let me go. The decision was one of the hardest we had to make. Being a father was the only thing more important to me than her.

The family I remembered was gone. Victoria was just thirteen when I left, but she wasn't a child anymore. She would turn eighteen in less than a month when I returned. Benjamin had turned into a sixteen-year-old young man, and Hugo was less than two years behind him. I'd lost their childhoods, so the best I could do was spend time with them now. I made them sandwiches for their lunch boxes and took them to school in the morning. I cooked their suppers, washed their clothes, and tried to tuck them into bed at night. They were too old for all of that.

The boys did accept me again. Victoria couldn't. That was my price to pay. I couldn't fix time or rewind my decisions. I did make peace with Charlotte though. We ended up like best friends. Even my dogs remembered and loved me.

Farsund led me to MIT. I began studying there soon after returning to the States, but I'd applied at the beginning of 2012 as I readied myself to move back. My five-year experience facing off against the auto giants gave me enough credibility for them to accept me.

MIT represented a future I longed for and something that finally had nothing to do with the German auto giants. I was born in Cambridge, UK, when my dad was earning his doctorate. I had always wanted to study there, like him. I wanted to show him I had tried to be all I could be; to be good enough. MIT is in Cambridge too—Massachusetts.

Recommendation letters are an important part of their admission requirements. I asked Richard Buch, the new Mayor of Farsund, if he would recommend me. Since universities value blind endorsements more, I never saw the contents of the letter he agreed to write until I graduated in 2014. Hilde sent me an email with a copy of the letter as a congratulatory gift. I found out it was written by Buch as well as another former mayor: Hilde's father.

January 2012
Firstly, we would like to present ourselves. We are Richard Ivar Buch, current Mayor of Farsund, Norway, and Ove Rullestad, former Mayor of Farsund. Farsund is a small town with almost three thousand inhabitants in the town and ten thousand inhabitants in the larger community.

Mr. Cockroft is the CEO of Farsund Aluminium Casting. He came to Farsund in 2007 to solve issues at a time when this casting company had great financial problems, and it later went bankrupt when the recession hit the European industries. Mr. Cockroft managed within a few months to save the company. During that time Mr. Cockroft achieved becoming the hero of all the workers and the inhabitants of Farsund for saving two hundred jobs plus all the side effects that are important in a small community.

By saving the company and a significant number of jobs, Mr. Cockroft has without doubt had an impact on a whole community. Wherever we go in Farsund we get positive feedback about him. He is perceived as a charismatic, open, and inviting person. And this is exactly how we see him.

I hope I made you proud, Dad.

Endnotes

CHAPTER 13: THE DARK DEMONS

1. Sneha Kamble and Sonia Mutreja, "Luxury Car Market," Allied Market Research, accessed July 18, 2023, https://www.alliedmarketresearch.com/luxury-car-market-A05980#.

2. Tom Huddleston, Jr., "This 1950s Roadster Nearly Bankrupted BMW, Now the Car Sells for Millions," Make It, CNBC, August 2, 2020, https://www.cnbc.com/2020/08/02/bmw-507-nearly-bankrupted-the-brand-now-sells-for-millions.html#.

3. Tom Buerkle, "BMW Wrests Rolls-Royce Name Away from VW," *International Herald Tribune,* July 29, 1998, https://www.nytimes.com/1998/07/29/news/bmw-wrests-rollsroyce-name-away-from-vw.html.

4. Jens Meiners, "The Car Guy Wins: Porsche CEO Wendelin Wiedeking Forced Out," *Car & Driver,* July 23, 2009, https://www.caranddriver.com/news/a18743091/the-car-guy-wins-porsche-ceo-wendelin-wiedeking-forced-out/.

5. Sören Amelang, and Benjamin Wehrmann, "'Dieselgate'—A Timeline of the Car Emissions Fraud Scandal in Germany," Clean Energy Wire, May 25, 2020,

https://www.cleanenergywire.org/factsheets/dieselgate-timeline-car-emissions-fraud-scandal-germany.

6. Bloomberg, "VW, Mercedes Suffer Blow in German Legal Fight Over Cheat Software in Diesels," *Europe Auto News*, June 26, 2023, https://europe.autonews.com/automakers/german-court-rules-automakers-must-pay-diesel-cheat-devices.

7. Roger Parloff, "How VW Paid $25 Billion for 'Dieselgate'—and Got Off Easy," Propublica, February 26, 2018, https://www.propublica.org/article/how-vw-paid-25-billion-for-dieselgate-and-got-off-easy.

8. Edward Taylor, "Volkswagen Says Diesel Scandal Has Cost It 31.3 Billion Euros." Reuters, March 17, 2020, https://www.reuters.com/article/us-volkswagen-results-diesel/volkswagen-says-diesel-scandal-has-cost-it-31-3-billion-euros-idUSKBN2141JB.

9. Marine Strauss and Alexander Hübner, "EU Fines Volkswagen, BMW $1 Bln for Emissions Cartel," Reuters, July 8, 2021, https://www.reuters.com/business/autos-transportation/eu-fines-bmw-volkswagen-group-restricting-competition-emission-cleaning-2021-07-08/#.

10. Sean O'Kane, "Daimler Fined Nearly $1 billion for Selling Cars That Cheated Emissions Tests," The Verge, September 24, 2019, https://www.theverge.com/2019/9/24/20881603/daimler-dieselgate-mercedes-benz-emissions-cheating-fine.

11. Aivaras Grigelevicius, "Who Makes the Most Reliable German Cars?" *Car Vertical* (Blog), May 25, 2022, https://www.carvertical.com/blog/who-makes-the-most-reliable-german-cars#.

12. Jill Petzinger, "Volkswagen Boss Herbert Diess Is Germany's Highest Paid CEO," Yahoo Finance, July 15,

2020, https://www.yahoo.com/video/volkswagen-boss-herbert-diess-is-germanys-highest-paid-ceo-085230575.html.

CHAPTER 14: FIVE BOMBS

1. Ben S. Bernanke, *Courage to Act: A Memoir of a Crisis and Its Aftermath* (New York: W. W. Norton and Company, 2017).
2. Luca Ciferri, "BMW Warns It Could Lose Money in 2009," *Automotive News Europe*, March 18, 2009, https://europe.autonews.com/article/20090318/ANE/303189974/bmw-warns-it-could-lose-money-in-2009.

CHAPTER 24: RECALL

1. Deisy Ventura, "Approximately How Many Parts Are in a Car on Average?" MotorBiscuit, May 21, 2023, https://www.motorbiscuit.com/approximately-many-parts-car-average/.
2. Nico Hooiveld, "Traceability in Automotive: What Decision-Makers and Experts Should Look Out for Now," Omron, May 23, 2022, https://industrial.omron.eu/en/solutions/blog/traceability-in-automotive.
3. Ben Lutkevich, "Bill of Materials (BOM)," TechTarget ERP, accessed August 1, 2023, https://www.techtarget.com/searcherp/definition/bill-of-materials-BoM?Offer=abt_pubpro_AI-Insider.
4. Nico Hooiveld, "Traceability in Automotive: What Decision-Makers and Experts Should Look Out for Now," Omron, May 23, 2022, https://industrial.omron.eu/en/solutions/blog/traceability-in-automotive.
5. Ben Lutkevich, "Bill of Materials (BOM)," TechTarget ERP, accessed August 1, 2023, https://

www.techtarget.com/searcherp/definition/
bill-of-materials-BoM?Offer=abt_pubpro_AI-Insider.

6. Nico Hooiveld, "Traceability in Automotive: What
Decision-Makers and Experts Should Look Out for Now,"
Omron, May 23, 2022, https://industrial.omron.eu/en/
solutions/blog/traceability-in-automotive.

7. Ben Lutkevich, "Bill of Materials (BOM),"
TechTarget ERP, accessed August 1, 2023, https://
www.techtarget.com/searcherp/definition/
bill-of-materials-BoM?Offer=abt_pubpro_AI-Insider.

8. The National Highway Traffic Safety Administration
(NHTSA), "Office of Defects Investigation (ODI)
Consumer Complaint Database of Complaints Reported
to NHTSA That Are Related to Firestone ATX, Wilderness,
and Other Tire Models Under Investigation as Part of
Engineering Analysis EA00-023," October 4, 2001, https://
icsw.nhtsa.gov/nhtsa/announce/press/firestone/Update.
html.

9. Kevin M. McDonald, "Separations, Blow-Outs, and
Fallout: A Treadise on the Regulatory Aftermath of
the Ford-Firestone Tire Recall," *The John Marshall Law
Review* 37, no. 4 (Summer): 1073–1179, accessed July 21,
2023, https://repository.law.uic.edu/lawreview/vol37/
iss4/2/.

10. The National Highway Traffic Safety Administration
(NHTSA), "Office of Defects Investigation (ODI)
Consumer Complaint Database of Complaints Reported
to NHTSA That Are Related to Firestone ATX, Wilderness,
and Other Tire Models Under Investigation as Part of
Engineering Analysis EA00-023," October 4, 2001, https://
icsw.nhtsa.gov/nhtsa/announce/press/firestone/Update.
html.

11. Kevin M. McDonald, "Separations, Blow-Outs, and Fallout: A Treadise on the Regulatory Aftermath of the Ford-Firestone Tire Recall," *The John Marshall Law Review* 37, no. 4 (Summer): 1073–1179, accessed July 21, 2023, https://repository.law.uic.edu/lawreview/vol37/iss4/2/.

12. The National Highway Traffic Safety Administration (NHTSA), "Office of Defects Investigation (ODI) Consumer Complaint Database of Complaints Reported to NHTSA That Are Related to Firestone ATX, Wilderness, and Other Tire Models Under Investigation as Part of Engineering Analysis EA00-023," October 4, 2001, https://icsw.nhtsa.gov/nhtsa/announce/press/firestone/Update.html.

13. Kevin M. McDonald, "Separations, Blow-Outs, and Fallout: A Treadise on the Regulatory Aftermath of the Ford-Firestone Tire Recall," *The John Marshall Law Review* 37, no. 4 (Summer): 1073–1179, accessed July 21, 2023, https://repository.law.uic.edu/lawreview/vol37/iss4/2/.

14. Ibid.

15. The National Highway Traffic Safety Administration (NHTSA), "Office of Defects Investigation (ODI) Consumer Complaint Database of Complaints Reported to NHTSA That Are Related to Firestone ATX, Wilderness, and Other Tire Models Under Investigation as Part of Engineering Analysis EA00-023," October 4, 2001, https://icsw.nhtsa.gov/nhtsa/announce/press/firestone/Update.html.

16. Kevin M. McDonald, "Separations, Blow-Outs, and Fallout: A Treadise on the Regulatory Aftermath of the Ford-Firestone Tire Recall," *The John Marshall Law*

Review 37, no. 4 (Summer): 1073–1179, accessed July 21, 2023, https://repository.law.uic.edu/lawreview/vol37/iss4/2/.

17. The National Highway Traffic Safety Administration (NHTSA), "Office of Defects Investigation (ODI) Consumer Complaint Database of Complaints Reported to NHTSA That Are Related to Firestone ATX, Wilderness, and Other Tire Models Under Investigation as Part of Engineering Analysis EA00-023," October 4, 2001, https://icsw.nhtsa.gov/nhtsa/announce/press/firestone/Update.html.

18. Kevin M. McDonald, "Separations, Blow-Outs, and Fallout: A Treadise on the Regulatory Aftermath of the Ford-Firestone Tire Recall," *The John Marshall Law Review* 37, no. 4 (Summer): 1073–1179, accessed July 21, 2023, https://repository.law.uic.edu/lawreview/vol37/iss4/2/.

19. The National Highway Traffic Safety Administration (NHTSA), "Office of Defects Investigation (ODI) Consumer Complaint Database of Complaints Reported to NHTSA That Are Related to Firestone ATX, Wilderness, and Other Tire Models Under Investigation as Part of Engineering Analysis EA00-023," October 4, 2001, https://icsw.nhtsa.gov/nhtsa/announce/press/firestone/Update.html.

20. Kevin M. McDonald, "Separations, Blow-Outs, and Fallout: A Treadise on the Regulatory Aftermath of the Ford-Firestone Tire Recall," *The John Marshall Law Review* 37, no. 4 (Summer): 1073–1179, accessed July 21, 2023, https://repository.law.uic.edu/lawreview/vol37/iss4/2/.

CHAPTER 28: THE WRATH OF ROTH

1. Current Procurement. "Lieferantenkrise: Unverhofft kommt nicht oft" (Interview with Martin Roth). September 1, 2010, https://beschaffung-aktuell.industrie.de/allgemein/lieferantenkrise-unverhofft-kommt-nicht-oft/.

CHAPTER 31: FLIP OF A COIN

1. Current Procurement. "Lieferantenkrise: Unverhofft kommt nicht oft" (Interview with Martin Roth)." September 1, 2010, https://beschaffung-aktuell.industrie.de/allgemein/lieferantenkrise-unverhofft-kommt-nicht-oft/.

Acknowledgments

___

I think everyone should write a book. It's kind of therapeutic, but bloody-hell, it takes a long time and a lot of help. That's why I want to thank those who were patient and put up with all my bullshit.

I had three different coaches at different stages of my evolving ability to write. It's not their words, they didn't scribe my book, but they did tell me what was crap and how to fix it. Thank you, R. Paulo Delgado, Kim Eldredge, and, most especially, Andrina Tran.

The team at Manuscripts LLC are very professional too. Publishing a book isn't an obvious process. Thanks for guiding me through this and making it real. I guess I've got to thank you for making me kill all my darlings too.

Finally I've got to thank those who were gullible enough to agree to read my draft manuscripts. I promised them I would. So thank you, Barb Cook and Rob Schott, but I have to thank Bettina Cockroft the most. She was forced into reading it twice. I owe you all a gin and tonic... all right, two.